$\mathcal{H}$APPY HATS
AND COOL CAPS

Anne-Mette Hermansen
Tina Elnef

$\mathcal{H}$APPY HATS AND **COOL CAPS**

to Sew for the Whole Family

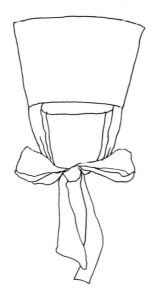

LARK BOOKS
Asheville, North Carolina

DRAWINGS: Anne-Mette Hermansen
PHOTOS: Jo Selsing
COVER DESIGN: Ole Morten Nygård

ART DIRECTOR: Chris Bryant
EDITOR: Dawn Cusick
TRANSLATOR: Robin Orm Hansen
PRODUCTION ASSISTACE: Hannes Charen
EDITORIAL ASSISTANCE: Evans Carter

Library of Congress Cataloging-in-Publication Data
Hermansen, Anne-Mette.
  [Huer og hatte til born og voksne. English]
  Happy hats and cool caps to sew for the whole family /
Anne-Mette Hermansen, Tina Elnef.
    p. cm.
  Includes index.
  ISBN 1-57990-026-7 (pbk.)
  ISBN 1-57990-075-5 (hbk.)
  1. Millinery.   2. Hats.   3. Caps (Headgear).   I. Elnef, Tina.   II. Title.
  TT655.H47   1998
  646.5' 04 —dc21   97-52392
                                                     CIP

10 9 8 7 6 5 4 3 2 1

Published by Lark Books
50 College Street
Asheville, North Carolina 28801, USA

Originally published as Huer Og Hatte Til Born Og Voksne, Borgens Forlag, 1994

English translation © 1998, Lark Books

Distributed by Random House, Inc., in the United States, Canada,
the United Kingdom, Europe, and Asia

Distributed in Australia by Capricorn Link (Australia) Pty Ltd.,
P.O. Box 6651, Baulkham Hills Business Centre, NSW 2153, Australia

Distributed in New Zealand by Tandem Press Ltd., 2 Rugby Rd.,
Birkenhead, Auckland, New Zealand

Every effort has been made to ensure that all the information in this book is accurate. However, due
to differing conditions, tools, and individual skills, the publisher cannot be responsible for any injuries,
losses, or other damages that may result from the use of the information in this book.

Printed in Hong Kong
All rights reserved
ISBN 1-57990-026-7 (pbk.)
ISBN 1-57990-075-5 (hbk.)

CONTENTS

INTRODUCTION

We've written this book for you because, like us, you like to wear hats or can use caps that are functional, warm, and festive.

Making hats and caps is fun—something even a beginner can do well. You needn't be an expert sewer to be able to use this book, as long as you read the first section, Using this Book, before you start, then follow the sewing directions for each design.

Most of the designs can be made of fabric remnants, so check your scrap bag before going to the store. The designs can be varied by your choice of fabric, accessories, or just about anything else your imagination fancies.

Dig in and have fun!

Anne-Mette Hermansen and Tina Elnef

USING THIS BOOK

This book shows you how to make hats and caps for the smallest babies, school children, teenagers, and adults. For each design, we tell what sizes the pattern encompasses. To find the correct pattern size, you will first need to measure the head size (HS) of the person who is going to wear the cap or hat.

HOW TO MEASURE HEAD SIZES (HS)

Wrap a measuring tape around the head, over—not above—the upper halves of the ears as shown in Fig. a. Do not stretch the tape too tight. (There should be room for a finger between the forehead and the measuring tape.)

In the patterns, we have taken into account whether the cap or hat should fit loose or tight on the head, but the fit in your finished hat will also depend on the fabric you choose. The hat will seem smaller in a heavy, tightly woven fabric than in a thin, loosely woven fabric.

If the head size lies between two pattern sizes, it makes sense to choose the larger size.

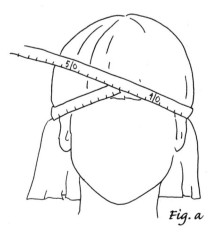

Fig. a

To avoid repeating ourselves, in many of the patterns we refer you to page 69, where you can find help with various sewing techniques, choosing fabrics, and so forth. Most of the hats in this book can be made with a small amount of fabric—a scrap or a remnant will usually do. The description for each cap or hat tells the yardage of fabric you will need based on 60-inch-wide (1.5 m) fabric; allow extra yardage if using a narrower fabric. Yardage given is for the largest size, unless otherwise indicated.

PRESHRINKING THE FABRIC

It's a good idea to launder and press fabrics, especially cotton and wool, before using them. This will prevent unhappy surprises with shrinkage on the finished hat.

FABRIC GRAIN AND CUTTING

It's important to be aware of the grain of the fabric, especially for stretch fabrics like jersey, fleece, and ribbed knits. In placing the pattern pieces on the fabric, be sure that the grain of the fabric corresponds to the grain indicated on the pattern piece. The *length* of the fabric as specified in the cutting directions always refers to the lengthwise grain direction; the width of a piece is always cut on the fabric cross grain. (See Fig. b.)

PRESSING

You can use an ordinary ironing board for pressing seams open, but a pressing ham gives the best results in pressing curves.

HAT ANATOMY

In the book we use the terms ***crown***, ***stand***, ***brim***, and ***visor***. Fig. c shows how these terms apply to various kinds of hats.

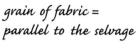

Fig. b

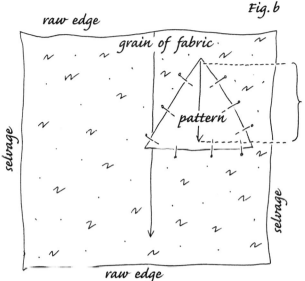

raw edge

grain of fabric

selvage

pattern

selvage

raw edge

grain of fabric =
parallel to the selvage

MAKING THE HATS

The sewing directions for each design give the construction order, step by step, with page references to the Sewing Tips section. The degree of difficulty is indicated by one, two, or three little caps following the title of each design.

The hats are generally easy to make, but we recommend you start with a one-cap design if you don't have a lot of sewing experience.

THE PATTERNS

In the back of the book you will find a pattern sheet. Designs 1–12 are on page 1; Designs 13–23 are on page 2.

We have used the following abbreviations throughout the book:

HS – Head size

CF – Center front of the cap or hat

CB – Center back of the cap or hat

Seam allowances are not included in the pattern pieces. Unless indicated otherwise, always leave a 3/8-inch (1 cm) seam allowance outside the paper pattern.

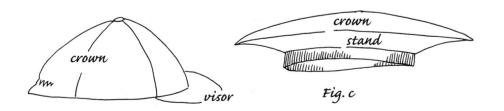

crown

stand

brim

crown

visor

crown

stand

Fig. c

BALACLAVA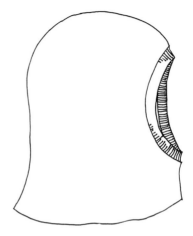

Balaclavas fit closely and are wonderfully warm. For use in moderately cold weather, make it in lightweight wool or cotton jersey. Line it with fleece, stretch velour, or a wool knit for extra warmth in severe weather.

SIZES	I	II	III
HS IN INCHES	17³⁄₈–19	19–20¹⁄₂	20¹⁄₂–22¹⁄₈
HS IN CM	44–48	48–52	52–56

MATERIALS
- ¹⁄₂ yard (.45 m) fabric
- ¹⁄₈ yard (.11 m) ribbing

PATTERN PIECES
1a, Balaclava: Cut two, one left and one right

CUTTING LAYOUT

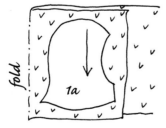

CONSTRUCTION

1. Pin pattern pieces to fabric. Mark CF and CB, and cut out, adding ³⁄₈ inch (1 cm) seam allowance on all edges.

2. Pin the pieces with right sides together. Sew up the back to the face opening and under the chin at CF with a narrow zigzag stitch or stretch stitch. Alternatively, overcast the seam allowances.

3. Overcast the lower edge. Turn under ³⁄₄ inch (2 cm) and hem, using a double needle if desired (page 65).

4. Cut the ribbing to measure the HS minus 3¹⁄₈ inches (8 cm) long and 2 inches (5 cm) wide. (Seam allowances are included.) Sew the short ends with right sides together (see page 72). Pin the ribbing to the face edge, right sides together, matching ribbing seam to chin seam. Sew with a narrow zigzag stitch or stretch stitch.

5. As an alternative, topstitch the ribbing seam allowance toward the hat using a double needle.

Variations

BALACLAVA WITH DINOSAUR CREST

PATTERN PIECES

1a, Balaclava: Cut two, one left and one right
1b, Dinosaur Crest: Cut 14

CONSTRUCTION

1. Cut out 14 dinosaur crest pieces, adding 3/8 inch (1 cm) seam allowance on all sides.

2. Place the pieces with right sides together to make seven pairs. Sew each pair together along the two curved edges.

3. Trim seam allowances, turn right side out, and press lightly.

4. Pin the crest pieces along the back edge on the right side of one balaclava piece, points inward as shown. Lay the other piece on top, wrong side up, sandwiching the triangles between as shown in Fig. 1.

5. Follow the directions for the Balaclava on the preceding page.

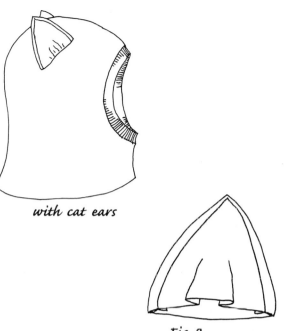

with cat ears

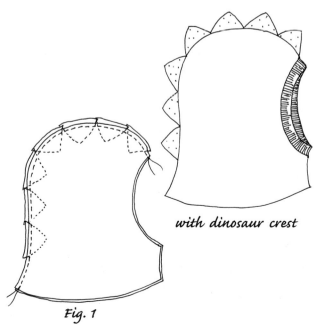

with dinosaur crest

Fig. 1

Fig. 2

BALACLAVA WITH CAT EARS

PATTERN PIECES:

1a, Balaclava: Cut two, one left and one right
1c, Cat Ears: Cut two each from two fabrics

CONSTRUCTION

1. Cut outer and inner ear pattern pieces from fabric, adding 3/8 inch (1 cm) seam allowance on all edges. Mark ear locations on hat pieces.

2. Pin the two parts of each ear with right sides together and sew the outer edges. Trim.

3. Turn right side out, fold the inner ear as shown in Fig. 2 and pin.

4. Turn the lower 3/8 inch (1 cm) of each ear to the inside. Pin the ears to the balaclava as marked, and sew in place by hand (page 74).

5. Follow the Balaclava construction steps on page 10.

LINED BALACLAVA

PATTERN PIECES

1a, Balaclava

CONSTRUCTION

1. Pin pattern pieces to the outer fabric and to the lining (see Fig. 3) to get a left and a right in each fabric. Cut out, adding ⅜ inch (1 cm) seam allowance on all edges.

2. Pin the outer cap pieces with right sides together. Sew the back and CF chin seam with a narrow zigzag stitch or stretch stitch. Sew lining pieces the same way.

3. Cut ribbing HS minus 3⅛ inches (8 cm) wide and 2 inches (5 cm) long. Sew the short ends with right sides together (page 72). Fold the ribbing in half and pin to the face opening of the outer hat with right sides together and raw edges aligned, matching the ribbing seam to the chin seam of the hat. Place the hat inside the lining with right sides together and the ribbing sandwiched between. Sew all three together with a narrow zigzag stitch or stretch stitch. Turn right side out.

4. Hem the lower edge by turning up both bottom edges ⅜ inch (1 cm) toward the wrong side. Topstitch close to the edge with a double needle or sew closed by hand (page 74).

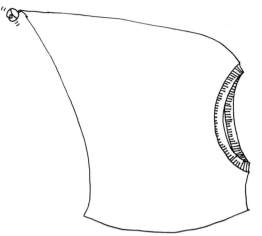

pointed balaclava with bell

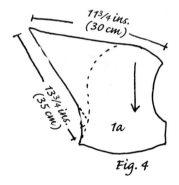

Fig. 4

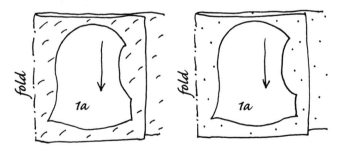

Fig. 3

BALACLAVA WITH POINTED HOOD

PATTERN PIECES

1 a, Balaclava: Cut two, one left and one right, altered as shown

CONSTRUCTION

1. Adjust the pattern as illustrated in Fig. 4.

2. Pin the pattern to the fabric and cut, adding ⅜ inch (1 cm) seam allowance on all edges.

3. Follow the Balaclava construction steps on page 10. Sew a bell, tassel, (page 59), or pompon (page 71) onto the point.

Left: Balaclava, page 10. *Right:* Balaclava with dinosaur crest, page 11.

JESTER'S HAT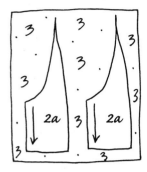

CUTTING LAYOUT

Make this cute, distinctive hat in two different colors or patterns of a brushed knit, flannel, jersey, or fleece. A band of ribbing keeps the hat snugly on the head.

SIZES	I	II
HS IN INCHES	19–20½	20½–22⅛
HS IN CM	48–52	52–56

MATERIALS

- ½ yard (.45 m) each of 2 different fabrics
- ⅛ yard (.11 m) ribbing
- Scrap yarn for tassels

PATTERN PIECES

2 a, Jester's Cap: Cut 4 if using one fabric or 2 each from two different fabrics.

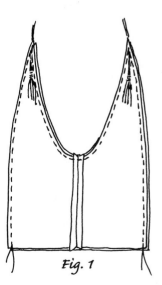

Fig. 1

CONSTRUCTION

1. Pin the pattern pieces to the fabric and mark CF and CB on each piece. Cut out, adding a ³⁄₈-inch (1 cm) seam allowance on all edges.

2. Pin fabric A to fabric B along CF with right sides together. Sew with a narrow zigzag stitch or stretch stitch.

3. Pin fabric A to fabric B along CB with right sides together. Sew with a short zigzag stitch or stretch stitch.

4. Make two tassels (page 59) by winding 20 turns around a piece of cardboard 2½ inches (6 cm) wide.

5. Pin fronts to backs with right sides together. Pin a tassel inside each point, sandwiching them between the two layers with the tassel end inward. Sew the sides, points, and the top curve between the points (see Fig. 1), taking care not to sew into the tassel itself.

6. Cut the ribbing to measure the HS minus 4 inches (10 cm) long and 3⅛ (8 cm) wide. (Seam allowance is included.) Pin to the edge of the cap with right sides facing and stitch (page 72). Zigzag across the seam allowance.

7. Turn the cap right side out. If desired, topstitch the ribbing to the cap with a double needle.

Variation

JE/TER'/ CAP WITH EARFLAP/

PATTERN PIECES
4 b, Earflap: Cut 4

CONSTRUCTION

1. Cut out earflaps, adding ³⁄₈ inch (1 cm) seam allowance on all edges.

2. Follow construction steps 1–5 from the Jester's Cap, page 15.

3. Follow construction steps 3 6 for the Inca Hat, page 17.

with pompon

with bow

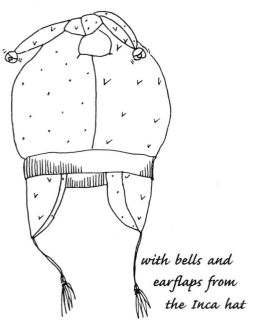

*with bells and
earflaps from
the Inca hat*

Left: Pointed Hat, page 20. *Center:* Inca Hat, page 17. *Right:* Jester's Hat, page 14.

INCA HAT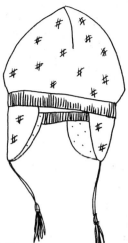

The big ear flaps keep a child's ears and cheeks warm and the winter wind at bay. Jersey, fleece, and stretch velour make good fabric choices.

SIZES	I	II
HS IN INCHES	17³/₄–19³/₄	19³/₄–21³/₄
HS IN CM	45 50	50–55

MATERIALS
- ¼ yard (.25 m) outer fabric
- ¼ yard lining fabric
- ⅛ yard (.11 m) ribbing
- ½ yard (.45 m) ribbon or yarn for tassels

PATTERN PIECES
4a, Crown: Cut 1 in outer fabric
4b, Earflaps: Cut 2 in outer fabric and 2 in lining fabric

CONSTRUCTION

1. Pin the pattern pieces to the fabric, marking CF and CB, and cut out with a ³/₈-inch (1 cm) seam allowance on all edges.

2. Pin the crown pieces together with right sides facing and sew with a short zigzag or stretch seam. Follow steps 4, 5, and 6 of the Cross Country Ski Cap on page 55, sewing the CB seam last.

3. Pin the ear flaps together, outer to inner with the right sides facing. If there is going to be a tassel (page 59) on the end or a tie (page 70), pin them sandwiched between the layers of ear flaps, tassel end in (see Fig. 1), and sew them in as you go. Sew the curve. Notch the seam allowance (page 70) and turn right side out.

CUTTING LAYOUT

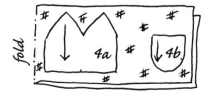

Fig. 1

4. Cut the ribbing to measure the HS minus 4 inches (10 cm) long by 3 inches (8 cm) wide. (Includes seam allowance.) Sew the ribbing together at the ends (page 72) and pin it to the hat, with the right sides facing and the ribbing seam matching the CB seam.

5. Pin the ear flaps, right sides facing, to the ribbing and the cap according to the pattern markings so that the rib is sandwiched between the ear flaps and the cap. Sew with a short zigzag or stretch seam. Optionally, zigzag the seam allowance. Turn right side out.

6. Optionally, topstitch the seam allowance to the hat.

with pompon

Variations

PIECED TOP SECTION

Cut the pattern in quarters, top to bottom. Add a ⅜-inch (1 cm) seam allowance on all edges and cut out the fabric. Piece the sections together as illustrated in Fig. 2.

EXTRA TALL HAT

Lengthen the pattern 1 to 2 inches (5–10 cm) at the bottom.

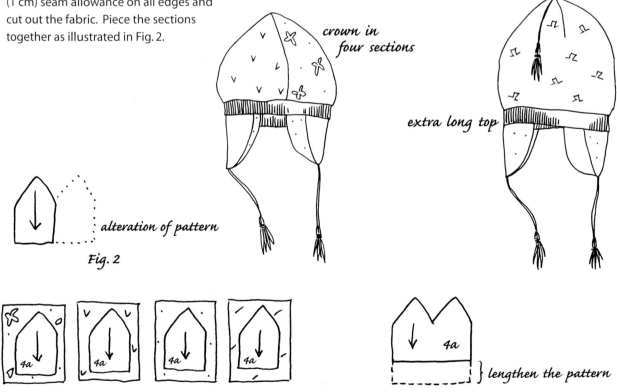

crown in four sections

extra long top

alteration of pattern

Fig. 2

} lengthen the pattern

BABY BONNET

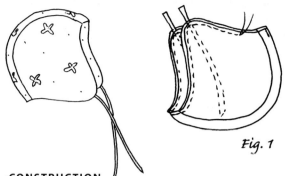

This lined, close-fitting bonnet is a classic for babies and toddlers. Choose jersey, fleece, stretch velour, or wool. For a winter cap, you might use wool as the outer fabric and cotton for the lining.

SIZES

	3 months	6 months	1 year

MATERIALS

- ⅓ yard (.35 m) outer fabric
- ⅓ yard lining fabric
- Optional: 2 pieces of 10-inch-long (25 cm) ribbon for ties

PATTERN PIECES

5a, Top Panel: Cut 1 each of outer and lining fabric
5b, Side Panels: Cut 2 each from outer and lining fabric

CUTTING LAYOUT

lining

Fig. 1

CONSTRUCTION

1. Pin pattern to the outer fabric. Transfer all markings to fabric, mark CF and CB, and cut out with ⅜-inch (1 cm) seam allowance on all edges. Repeat in lining fabric.

2. Pin the outer fabric's side panels to the long edges of the top panel with right sides facing, from markings A to B. Sew with a short zigzag or a stretch seam. Repeat this step in the lining fabric.

3. Make two 10-inch-long ties from fabric strips (page 70) if not using ribbon ties.

4. Pin ties to the point of the ear flaps, long ends in, and place the bonnet and lining together, right sides facing, with the ties sandwiched between them as shown in Fig. 1. Pin edges together and sew with a zigzag or a stretch seam, leaving about 3 inches (8 cm) open at CB.

5. Turn right side out through the opening and hand sew the opening closed (page 74).

6. Optionally, topstitch along the edge and/or sew a little zigzag overlapping the very edge for a sweet, scalloped effect on the edge.

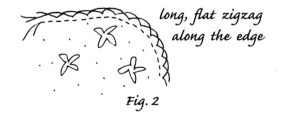

long, flat zigzag along the edge

Fig. 2

POINTED HAT

A good hat for any day, but especially for Halloween and other fun times. You can make it in a number of elastic fabrics—fleece, stretch velour, jersey, or cotton lycra. An inside band of ribbing helps keep the hat in place.

SIZES

HS IN INCHES	9½–21½
HS IN CM	50–55 cm

MATERIALS

- ½ yard (.45 m) of fabric A
- ⅓ yard (.35 m) of fabric B
- ⅛ yard (.11 m) ribbing
- Yarn scrap for pompon

PATTERN PIECES

6a, Crown: Cut 1 from fabric A
6b, Brim: Cut 2 from fabric B

CUTTING LAYOUT

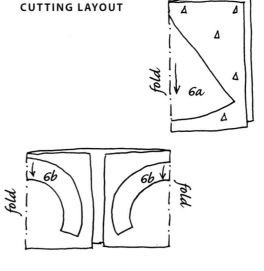

with Inca ear flaps

CONSTRUCTION

1. Pin pattern pieces to fabric and mark CF and CB. Add a 3/8-inch (1 cm) seam allowance on all edges and cut fabric.

2. Fold the crown lengthwise with right sides facing, and sew the long sides together with a short zigzag stitch or a stretch seam. Turn right side out.

3. Fold one brim piece with right sides facing, and sew the CB seam. Repeat with the other brim piece.

4. Pin the two brim pieces together with right sides facing and sew the outer edges together. Trim the seam allowance.

5. Turn right side out, press the edge flat, and topstitch close to the edge.

6. Cut the ribbing to measure the HS minus 2¾ inches (7 cm) long by 4 inches (10 cm) wide (includes seam allowance). Fold the ribbing (page 72) and sew the ends together.

7. Mark CF and CB on the crown and on the brim.

8. Place the base of the crown inside the brim with right sides facing, matching the CF and CB points, then place the ribbing on the bottom of the brim and pin in place. (The brim's raw edge should be sandwiched between ribbing and crown.)

9. Sew through all three layers, stretching the rib to fit.

10. Make a pompon (page 71), and sew it by hand through both brim and crown as shown on preceding page.

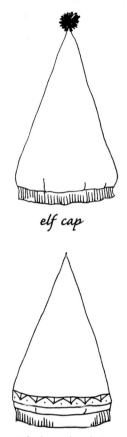

elf cap

with braid edging

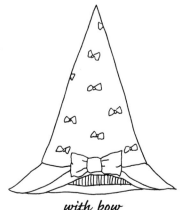

with bow

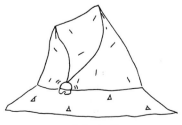

with bell

SAILOR HAT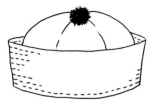

Here's a real seaman's hat with the crown and brim in a chunky fabric. The hat makes up best in canvas, denim, or heavy, colored cottons. If the fabric seems too thin, add iron-on interfacing to the wrong side before sewing.

quilted brim and tassel

SIZES	I	II	III
HS IN INCHES	19¾	20½	21¼
HS IN CM	50	52	54

MATERIALS
- ½ yard (.45 m) fabric
- Small button
- Yarn remnant for a pompon or tassel

PATTERN PIECES
7a, Crown: Cut 6
7b, Brim: Cut 2

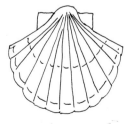

CUTTING LAYOUT

CONSTRUCTION

1. Pin pattern pieces to fabric and mark CF and CB. Add a ³/₈ inch (1 cm) seam allowance on all edges and cut out.

2. Fold the two brim pieces in half. Sew the CB seam on each separately with right sides facing.

3. Press the CB seam allowance and pin the brim pieces together with right sides facing, matching CB and CF.

4. Sew brim pieces together with right sides facing along the outer edge. Press seam allowances apart with an iron or your fingernail. Turn right side out.

5. Cover the brim with evenly spaced lines of topstitching, ³/₈ inch apart, starting ³/₈ inch from the outer edge.

6. Zigzag the edges of each of the 6 crown pieces.

7. Pin the crown pieces together three by three with right sides facing and sew together. Press the seam allowances apart.

8. Pin the two halves of the crown together with right sides facing and sew together. Press the seam allowances apart.

9. Stitch down all seam allowances on the crown. Sew from the inside, ¹/₄ inch (6 mm) from the seams as shown in Fig.1. Turn right side out.

10. Place the crown into the brim with right sides facing. Pin the brim's CB to a seam of the crown and CF to the opposite seam as shown in Fig. 2. Sew together. Zigzag the seam allowance.

11. Turn down the brim and stitch the seam allowance to the inside of the crown. Turn up the brim.

12. Make a pompon (page 71). Sew the pompon to the top of the crown, using a small button on the inside as reinforcement.

name on brim

beaded brim

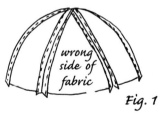

wrong side of fabric

Fig. 1

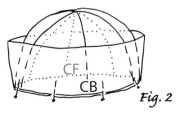

CF

CB

Fig. 2

Left to right: Sailor Hat, page 22; Soft Beret, page 28; Sahara Hat, page 27; and Afghan Farmer's Hat, page 46

BASEBALL CAP

A snappy cap for both children and adults. You can
make the cap in many different fabrics, including
cotton, open-weave linen, denim, corduroy, and leather.

SIZES	I	II	III	IV	V	VI
HS IN INCHES	19–20½	20½–22	22–23	23–23¾	23¾ 24½	24½–25¼
HS IN CM	48–52	52–56	56–58	58–60	60–62	62–64

with ear flaps

MATERIALS

- ½ yard (.45 m) fabric
- Heavy cardboard or plastic to reinforce the visor
- ⅔ yard (.65 m) bias tape or twill tape
- Button
- 3 inches (7 cm) of ⅜-inch-wide (1 cm) elastic

PATTERN PIECES

8a, Crown: Cut 2
8b, Crown: Cut 4
8c, Visor: Cut 2 in fabric and 1 in cardboard or plastic

CUTTING LAYOUT

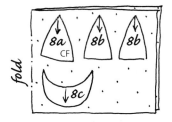

CONSTRUCTION

1. Pin the pattern pieces to the fabric and mark CF. Add a ⅜ inch (1 cm) seam allowance on all sides and cut out. Cut cardboard (or plastic) with no seam allowance.

2. Zigzag the two long sides on all six crown pieces.

3. Pin crown pieces 8b together in pairs, matching long sides and with right sides facing. Sew one long side on each pair. Press seam allowances apart.

4. Pin the long side of one crown piece 8a to the right side of one unit of 8b crown pieces with right sides facing. Pin a long side of the other 8a piece to the left side of the other 8b crown unit with right sides facing. (Refer to Fig. 1.) Sew together, then press seam allowances apart.

5. Pin the two crown units together with right sides facing, matching CF points. Sew the two units together in one seam, then press the seam allowances apart.

6. Topstitch all seam allowances to the crown, ¼ inch (6 mm) from the seams, working from the outside.

7. Pin the visor pieces together with right sides facing and sew the long curve.

8. Notch the curves (page 70). Trim seam allowance to ¼ inch. Turn right side out and press lightly.

9. Insert the cardboard or plastic into the fabric visor, taking care that the seam allowances inside lie smoothly on the same side of the cardboard.

10. Topstitch the stiffening material to the cloth visor with two seams, parallel to the outer edge of the visor and about ⅜ inch apart. (See Fig. 2.) Zigzag the inner edges together.

11. Pin the visor to the crown with right sides facing, matching CFs, and sew it on.

12. Pin the seam allowance to the inside lower edge of the cap. Mark the center of the elastic and pin it to the seam allowance at the back edge of the cap, starting at the CB and stretching it some in both directions. Keeping the elastic stretched, sew it in place with a little zigzag seam.

13. Pin a tape all the way around the lower edge of the cap on the inside, covering the seam allowance. Sew the tape to the cap's edge and press lightly. Sew a short seam across the tape at CB to hold the band in place.

14. Turn right side out and, if you wish, sew a button to the top center of the cap.

Fig. 1

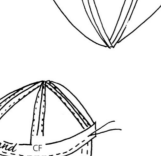

Fig. 3

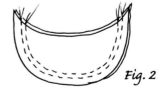

Fig. 2

Variation

SAHARA HAT

MATERIALS

- For the hat itself, see the materials list for the Baseball Cap
- For the neck shade, 1/4 yard (.2 m) fabric

PATTERN PIECES

For the hat itself, see the pattern section of the Baseball Cap

8d, Sahara Shade: Cut 1

CONSTRUCTION

1. Follow steps 1-12 for the Baseball Cap.

2. Pin and cut the Sahara Shade with a 3/8-inch (1 cm) seam allowance above and a 3/4-inch (2 cm) seam allowance on the lower curved edge. Mark CB.

3. Fold the lower edge up 3/8 inch toward the wrong side and press. Fold up another 3/8 inch and press again. Hem.

4. Zigzag the upper edge and baste in a gathering thread (page 73). Gather the Sahara Shade so that the upper edge fits the back edge of the cap from one end of the visor to the other as shown in Fig. 4.

5. Pin the Sahara Shade to the hat's lower edge with right sides facing and sew together. Turn seam allowance toward hat. Pin tape around the lower edge of hat, covering the seam allowance of the Sahara Shade. Stitch tape close to the lower edge. (Refer to Fig. 3.) Sew a short seam at CB across the tape to hold it in place.

6. Follow step 14 in the Baseball Cap's instructions.

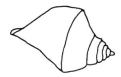

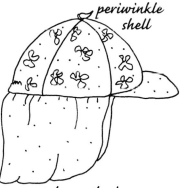

Sahara Shade

periwinkle shell

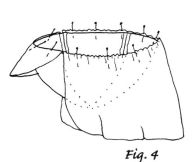

Fig. 4

SOFT BERET

This beret lies softly around the face and can be worn year 'round. You can make it in all sorts of fabrics. Try it in jersey, wool, fleece, or soft leathers.

SIZES	I	II	III	IV
HS IN INCHES	17³/₄–19¹/₂	19¹/₂–21³/₄	21³/₄–23¹/₂	23¹/₂–25¹/₄
HS IN CM	45–50	50–55	55–60	60–64

MATERIALS
- ¹/₂ yard (.45 m) fabric
- ¹/₈ yard (.11 m) ribbing

PATTERN PIECES
Use a compass to draw your own circular pattern on paper. (Or make your own compass as shown in Fig. 1.) Cut out the circle and fold in quarters to mark the grain of fabric.

SIZE I needs a radius of 7 inches (18 cm)

SIZE II needs a radius of 8 inches (20 cm)

SIZE III needs a radius of 8³/₄ inches (22 cm)

SIZE IV needs a radius of 9¹/₂ inches (24 cm)

with bow

with buttons

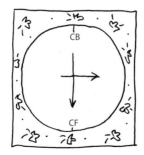

with pompon

crown divided into four sections

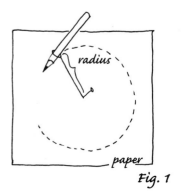

radius

paper

Fig. 1

CUTTING LAYOUT

CONSTRUCTION

1. Pin the pattern to fabric as shown at bottom of page 28. (Remember grain of fabric!) Mark CF and CB, add a ³⁄₈-inch (1 cm) seam allowance around the edge, and cut out.

2. Baste a gathering thread (page 73) ³⁄₈ inch from the edge of the circle.

3. Cut the ribbing to measure the HS minus 4 inches (10 cm) long by 3 inches (8 cm) wide (includes seam allowance). Sew the ribbing ends together.

4. Pull up the gathering thread to match HS. Pin ribbing to the edge of the hat (page 72) with right sides facing and with the seam on the ribbing matching the CB. Stretch the ribbing lightly to fit. Sew together with a short zigzag or stretch seam, stretching the ribbing lightly to fit as you sew.

Variations
BOW

1. Follow steps 1–4 of the Soft Beret.

2. Cut a band of fabric for the bow 4³⁄₄ inches (12 cm) wide and 54 inches (1.4 m) long, including seam allowance.

3. Fold, press, and sew the band together lengthwise with right sides facing, leaving an opening of HS minus 4³⁄₄ inches in the middle and sewing the ends diagonally. (Refer to Fig. 2.)

4. Trim the seam allowance closely at the ends and turn right side out.

5. Sew the ribbing ends together (page 72).

6. Pin the bow band to the circle's right side edge, leaving 4³⁄₄ inches of the hat circumference free (to be able to tie the bow) on one side of the crown. Pin the ribbing outside the band, sandwiching the seam allowance of the bow band between the crown and the ribbing as shown in Fig. 3.

7. Sew all the way around with a short zigzag or stretch seam, stretching the ribbing lightly to fit as you sew. Zigzag the seam allowances together. Turn right side out.

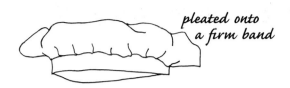

pleated onto a firm band

PLEATED WITH A WOVEN BAND

1. Draft and cut a crown as for the Soft Beret.

2. Cut a fabric band measuring the HS + ³⁄₄ inch (2 cm) long by 3 inches (8 cm) including seam allowance. Sew the ends together with right sides facing to form a ring. Press seam allowances apart, fold lengthwise in half, and press with the wrong sides facing.

3. Pin pleats into the edge of the circle—many small pleats or a few deep pleats, depending on the fabric—so that the edge of the circle exactly matches the band. Pin the band to the crown with right sides facing and sew together. Zigzag the seam allowance and turn it to the inside.

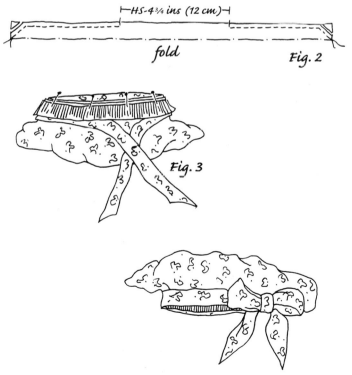

⊢HS-4³⁄₄ ins (12 cm)⊣

fold **Fig. 2**

Fig. 3

FLOPPY SUN HAT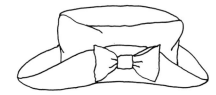

A soft hat with a soft brim. In raw silk, it's a summer party hat; in a light wool, a warm winter hat. Other suitable fabrics include velour, heavy cotton, corduroy, linen, fleece, leather, and pellon-backed burlap. Line with light cotton or silk.

SIZES	I	II	III	IV
HS IN INCHES	21¼–22	22–23	23–23½	23½–24½
HS IN CM	54–56	56–58	58–60	60–62

MATERIALS
- ⅝ yard (.55 m) outer fabric
- ⅓ yard (.35 m) lining fabric

PATTERN PIECES
11a, Crown: Cut 1 in outer fabric and 1 in lining
11b, Stand: Cut 1 in outer fabric and 1 in lining
11c, Brim: Cut 2 in outer fabric

CUTTING LAYOUT

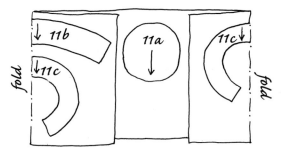

CONSTRUCTION

1. Pin pattern pieces on outer fabric and mark CF and CB. Add a ⅜-inch (1 cm) seam allowance on all edges and cut out. Repeat with lining fabric.

2. Pin the ends of the outer stand together with right sides facing and sew together. Pin the ends of the lining stand together and the two ends of each brim at CB. Sew separately, then press seam allowances apart.

3. Pin the two brims together with right sides facing and sew the outer edges. Notch the seam allowance if you are using a heavy fabric (page 70). Turn right side out and press lightly. Topstitch around the outer edge ¼ inch (½ cm) in. Pin the inside edges together.

4. Pin the lower edges of the outer and lining stands each to its own side of the brim with right sides facing, matching CB and CF points. Sew together along lower edge.

5. Pin the outer stand to the outer crown with right sides facing, matching CF and CB points. Sew together. Press seam allowances toward the stand. Topstitch the seam allowance onto the stand ¼ inch from the seam.

6. Pin the lining stand to the lining crown with right sides facing and sew together with a ¾-inch (1.5 cm) seam allowance. Leave 4 inches (10 cm) open for turning.

7. Turn right side out through the opening. Close the opening with small hand stitching (page 74). Smooth the lining into the outer crown.

8. Optionally, make a bow (page 74) and attach it at CF.

Left: Soft Beret with bow ribbon tie, page 29.   *Right:* Floppy Sun Hat, page 30.

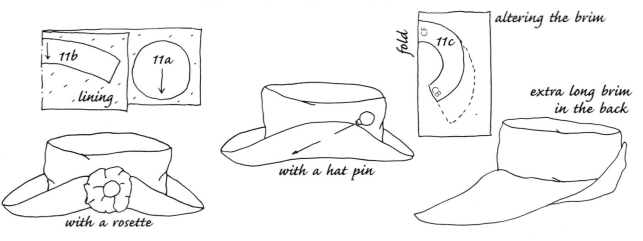

altering the brim

extra long brim in the back

with a hat pin

with a rosette

PILLBOX / HIP-HOP HAT

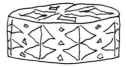

This simple hat has many different looks, depending on the fabric it's made from and the personality of its wearer. Try making the hat in cotton, linen, fleece, wool, leather, or heavy silk, with the lining in either light cotton or silk. You may even want to add some decorative embroidery.

SIZES	I	II	III
HS IN INCHES	20½–21¼	21¼–22	22–22¾
HS IN CM	52–54	54–56	56–58

SIZES	IV	V	VI
HS IN INCHES	22¾–23½	23½–24½	24½–25¼
HS IN CM	58–60	60–62	62–64

MATERIALS

- ⅓ yard (.35 m) outer fabric
- ⅓ yard lining fabric

PATTERN PIECES

12a, Crown: Cut 1 in outer fabric and 1 in lining fabric
12b, Stand: Cut 1 in outer fabric and 1 in lining fabric

CONSTRUCTION

1. Pin pattern pieces onto the outer fabric and mark CF and CB. Add a ⅜-inch (1 cm) seam allowance on all edges and cut out. Repeat with lining fabric.

2. Pin the ends of the outer stand together with right sides facing and sew together at CB. Press seam allowances apart.

3. Pin the outer crown to the outer stand with right sides facing, matching CF and CB. Sew together.

CUTTING LAYOUT

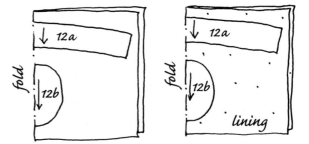

4. Press the seam allowance onto the stand and turn right side out. Topstitch seam allowance down ¼ inch (.5 cm) away from the seam on the stand.

5. Sew the lining together the same way, but with a ¾-inch (1.5 cm) seam allowance when attaching the crown to the stand. Don't stitch the seam allowance to the stand, and leave a 4-inch (10 cm) opening for turning.

6. Press the seam allowance of the lining onto the stand and turn right side out.

7. Pin the outer hat and lining together along the bottom edge with right sides facing, matching CB points. Sew together.

8. Turn right side out through the opening. Hand stitch the opening closed (page 74).

9. Press the lower edge lightly, then pin and topstitch ¼ inch from the edge.

with visor

zebra

leopard

beaded stand

appliqué

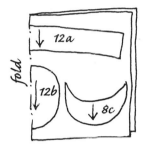

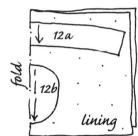

braid

pompon

Variation

WITH VISOR

MATERIALS
- All materials from Pillbox / Hip-Hop Hat
- Cardboard or plastic to stiffen the visor, 8 by 10 inches (20 by 25 cm)

PATTERN PIECES
12a, Crown: Cut 1 in outer fabric and 1 in lining fabric

12b, Stand: Cut 1 in outer fabric and 1 in lining fabric

8c, Visor (from Baseball Cap): Cut 2 in outer fabric and 1 in cardboard

CONSTRUCTION

1. Follow steps 1–6 for Pillbox / Hip-Hop Hat.

2. Pin the visor pattern to the outer fabric and mark the CF. Add a ³⁄₈ inch (1 cm) seam allowance on all edges and cut out.

3. Pin the visor together with right sides facing and sew the outer edges together.

4. Notch the seam allowance (page 70). Trim the seam allowance to ¹⁄₄ inch. Turn right side out and press lightly.

5. Cut out a cardboard or plastic visor (with no seam allowance) and place it inside the fabric visor, taking care that all of the seam allowance lies on the same side of the cardboard.

6. Sew two lines of topstitching along the outer edge of the visor about ³⁄₈ inch apart. Zigzag the inner edges of the visor together.

7. Pin visor to the stand with right sides facing, matching the CF points. Pin the lining to the stand with right sides facing, matching the CF points and sandwiching the visor between the outer fabric and the lining. Sew together.

8. Turn right side out through the opening. Sew the opening closed by hand (page 74).

9. Press the lower edge lightly. Optionally, topstitch ¹⁄₄ inch from the bottom edge.

Left: Grunge Cap, page 35. Center: Hip-Hop Hat, page 32. Right: Hip-Hop Hat with visor, page 33, and mittens, page 62.

GRUNGE CAP

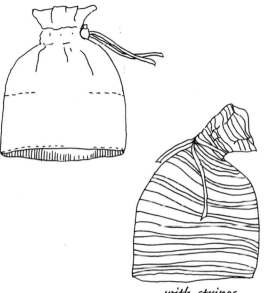

with stripes

The Grunge Cap is great for biking and skiing, and you can wear it in both city and country. The top can be opened to air the top of your head or pulled down around your neck as a neck warmer. Make it in a patterned fleece.

HAT SIZES

SMALL CHILDREN	HS by 11 ins. (28 cm) long
MEDIUM CHILDREN	HS by 11¾ ins. (30 cm) long
ADULTS	HS by 12½ ins. (32 cm) long

RIBBING SIZES

SMALL CHILDREN	HS minus 2⅓ ins. (6 cm) by 4 ins. (10 cm) long
MEDIUM CHILDREN	HS minus 2⅓ ins. by 4⅓ ins. (11 cm) long
ADULTS	HS minus 2⅓ ins. by 4¾ ins. (12 cm) long

Sizes include a ⅜-inch (1 cm) seam allowance.

MATERIALS
- ⅓ yard fabric
- ⅛ yard (.12 m) ribbing
- 32 inches (80 cm) nylon cord

PATTERN PIECES
See Sizes

CUTTING LAYOUT

cap piece

CONSTRUCTION

1. Measure the head for the cap piece (see Sizes) and cut out. (Note: A ⅜-inch seam allowance has already been included.) Zigzag all edges. Cut out ribbing (see Sizes).

2. Mark CF on the cap piece and the ribbing. Pin the parts together lengthwise with right sides facing. Sew together with a short zigzag or stretch seam, stretching the ribbing somewhat to fit.

3. Fold the cap together into a tube with right sides facing and pin together, taking care that the ends of the seam meet exactly. Begin sewing 2¾ inches (7 cm) from the upper edge of the cap and stop at the bottom of the ribbing as shown in Fig. 1.

4. Fold the seam allowance of the opening apart and stitch down. (See Fig. 2.)

5. Fold the top 1½ inches (4 cm) of the cap to the inside. Pin and stitch two seams, one ½ inch (1.5 cm) and the other

1⅓ inches (3.5 cm) from the folded edge to form a channel. (Refer to Fig. 3.)

6. Zigzag the lower raw edge of the ribbing. Fold the ribbing up into the cap at the seam. Pin and topstitch ⅜ inch from the edge.

7. Topstitch along the top of the ribbing to hold the upper edge of ribbing to the cap. Turn right side out.

8. Slip a piece of nylon cord through the channel and end with a cord clip, a bead, or a bow.

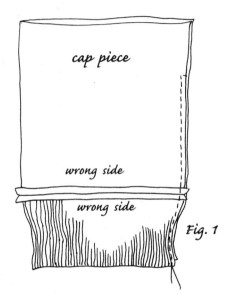

cap piece

wrong side

wrong side

Fig. 1

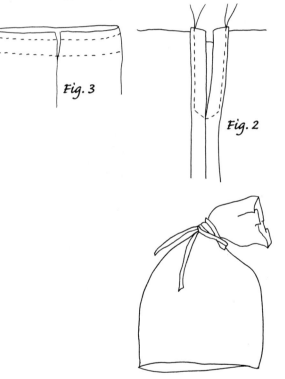

Fig. 3

Fig. 2

Variations
GRUNGE CAP WITHOUT RIBBING

1. Measure head for cap size (See Sizes) and add 4 inches (10 cm) to the length. Cut out. (A seam allowance is already included.) Zigzag all the way around.

2. Fold the cap crosswise with right sides facing and sew the CB seam with a short zigzag or a stretch seam.

3. Turn the bottom edge up ¾ inch (2 cm) to the inside and sew down.

4. Turn the top edge down ⅜ inch to the inside. Sew as in Step 3 above. Press the seams lightly.

5. Cut out a strip of fabric along the grain 1½ inches wide by 17¾ inches (45 cm) long. Sew lengthwise to make a tie (page 70).

6. Sew the middle of the tie to the cap at the CB, 3⅛ inch (8 cm) from the top.

7. Wrap the tie several times around the top of the cap and tie.

From left to right, back row: Ski Patrol Hat, page 56; Grunge Cap with Ribbing, page 35; Mittens, page 62.
From left to right, front row: Cross Country Ski Cap, page 54; Earwarmers, page 52.

From left to right: Squashy Cap, page 40; Russian Hat, page 53; Afghan Farmer's Hat, page 46; Hooded Shawl, page 60.

SIXPENCE

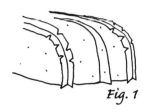

Fig. 1

This soft-crowned flat cap features a visor covered in the same fabric as the rest of the cap. Cotton, linen, light wools, leather, and corduroy work well for this design. For the lining, use light cottons, linen, or synthetic lining fabrics.

SIZES

SIZES	I	II	III
HS IN INCHES	$21^{1}/_{4}$–$22^{1}/_{8}$	$22^{1}/_{8}$–23	23–$23^{3}/_{4}$
HS IN CM	54–56	56–58	58–60

SIZES	IV	V
HS IN INCHES	$23^{3}/_{4}$–$24^{1}/_{2}$	$24^{1}/_{2}$–$25^{1}/_{4}$
HS IN CM	60–62	62–64

MATERIALS

• $^{1}/_{2}$ yard (.45 m) outer fabric
• $^{1}/_{2}$ yard lining fabric
• Cardboard or plastic to stiffen visor
• Snap fastener

PATTERN PIECES

9a, Top Panel: Cut 1 in outer fabric and 1 in lining fabric

9b, Stand: Cut 1 in outer fabric and 1 in lining fabric

9c, Visor: Cut 2 in outer fabric and 1 in cardboard or plastic with no seam allowance

CUTTING LAYOUT

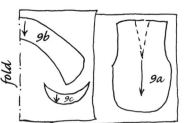

CONSTRUCTION

1. Pin the pattern pieces on the fabric and transfer the markings and CF and CB to fabric. Add a $^{3}/_{8}$-inch seam allowance on all edges and cut out. Repeat in lining fabric.

2. Pin the dart in the outer top panel with right sides facing and sew. Press the dart to left.

3. Pin the top to the stand with right sides facing, matching markings and CF. Sew together. Press seam allowances apart and notch the curves as shown in Fig. 1.

4. Pin the visor pieces together with right sides facing and matching the CF points. Sew together along the outside edge. Notch curve. Trim the seam allowance to $^{1}/_{4}$ inch (.5 cm). Turn the visor right side out and press lightly.

continued on page 41

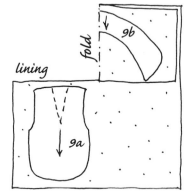

SQUASHY CAP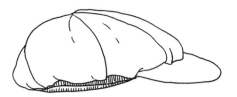

This hat can be worn in a variety of attractive ways: wear it cocked over one ear, turn it around so the visor's over the back of your neck, or pull it down around your ears. The big crown makes it roomy and the hat looks great made up in wool, velour, linen, and cottons.

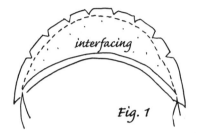

SIZES	I	II	III
HS IN INCHES	$19^3/_4$–$21^1/_4$	$21^1/_4$–23	23–$24^1/_2$
HS IN CM	50–54	54–58	58–62

Fig. 1

MATERIALS

- ½ yard (.45 m) outer fabric
- ½ yard lining fabric
- ⅓ yard (.30 m) iron-on interfacing
- ⅛ yard (.11 m) ribbing

PATTERN PIECES

10a, Crown: Cut 8 pieces each from outer and lining fabrics

10b, Visor: Cut 2 pieces in outer fabric and 4 pieces in interfacing

CUTTING LAYOUT

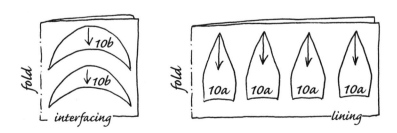

CONSTRUCTION

1. Pin the pattern pieces onto the outer fabric and mark the CF. Add a 3/8-inch (1 cm) seam allowance on all edges and cut out. Repeat in lining fabric. Cut out the interfacing without seam allowance.

2. Press 2 pieces interfacing, layered, on the wrong side of each visor piece, matching the edge of the interfacing with the seam lines of the fabric.

3. Pin the visor pieces together with right sides facing and sew along the outer curve of the interfacing as shown in Fig. 1. Notch the curve (page 70).

4. Turn right side out and press lightly. Topstitch along the outer edge, 3/8 inch in.

5. Pin the outer crown pieces together with right sides facing. Sew together in pairs, then make fours, and finally sew the two halves together. Press all seam allowances apart. Repeat the same steps with the lining crown.

6. Cut a piece of ribbing to the HS minus 6 inches (15 cm) long by 3 inches (8 cm) wide. Sew the ends of the ribbing together in a ring (page 72). Fold in half lengthwise, turn right side out, and mark off eight equal sections with pins.

7. Pin the visor to the outer crown with right sides facing, matching the CF points.

8. Pin ribbing to the right side of the lining crown, matching each pin to a seam and the ribbing seam to CB.

9. Pin the outer crown and lining crown together with right sides facing, sandwiching the visor and the ribbing between them. Optionally, baste this seam.

10. Sew all the way around 3/8 inch in, leaving a 4-inch (10 cm) opening at the CB.

11. Turn the cap right side out through the opening, then sew the opening closed by hand (page 74).

12. Optionally, cover a button with matching fabric and sew it to the center top of the cap.

continued from page 39

5. Cut out a visor in cardboard or plastic with no seam allowance and put it into the fabric visor, taking care that the seam allowance on the inside is on top of the cardboard. Set one half of the snap fastener into the top of the visor through both fabric and cardboard, as marked. The snap should be invisible from the underside of the visor.

6. Pin the dart in the lining top panel with right sides facing and sew. Press the dart to the left.

7. Sew the lining as in Step 3, but with a 1/2 inch (1.5 cm) seam allowance, sewing from A to B.

8. Pin visor to the outer fabric with right sides facing and following markings. Pin lining over the visor, sandwiching it with right sides facing and following the markings.

9. Sew the outer fabric and linings together with right sides facing along the lower edge, leaving a 3 1/2-inch (9 cm) opening on one side.

10. Turn right side out through the opening. Press the edge lightly and sew the opening closed by hand (page 74). Set the other half of the snap fastener in the stand, through both lining and outer fabrics, as marked. The stand can then be snapped to the visor, giving the six-pence its characteristic wedge-shaped profile.

ALPINE SKIMMER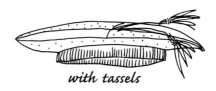

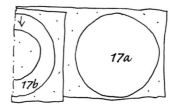

with buttons on the ribbing

with bow

with tassels

This festive beret can be made in the traditional manner or the crown can be divided into four or more sections. Make it in fleece, light wools, cotton, linen, or soft leather.

CUTTING LAYOUT

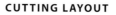

17b

17a

SIZES	I	II	III	IV
HS IN INCHES	17³/₄–19³/₄	19³/₄–21³/₄	21³/₄–23³/₄	23³/₄–25¹/₄
HS IN CM	45–50	50–55	55–60	60–64

CONSTRUCTION

1. Pin the pattern pieces on the fabric. Add a ³/₈-inch (1 cm) seam allowance on all edges and cut out.

2. Pin the crown and the stand together along the outer edge with right sides facing. Sew with a zigzag or a stretch stitch if the fabric is elastic. (Refer to Fig. 1.) Zigzag the

MATERIALS

- ¹/₃ yard (.30 m) fabric
- ¹/₈ yard (.11 m) ribbing
- HS minus 4 inches (10 cm) wide by 3 inches (8 cm) long of ribbing (includes seam allowance)

PATTERN PIECES

17a, Crown: Cut 1
17b, Stand: Cut 1

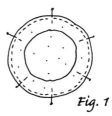

Fig. 1

seam allowance and notch the curves (page 70). Turn right side out and press lightly.

3. Topstitch the seam allowance to the crown, about ¼ inch (.5 cm) in from the seam as shown in Fig. 2.

4. Cut the ribbing to measure the HS minus 4 inches (10 cm) long by 3 inches (8 cm) wide. (Includes seam allowance.) Pin and sew the ribbing to the inside circle of the stand with right sides facing (page 72).

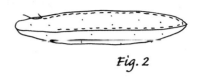

Fig. 2

in four sections

Variation

ALPINE SKIMMER DIVIDED BY 4

1. Fold and cut the pattern pieces for the crown in quarters. Pin pieces to the fabric (two or more colors) and cut out with a ⅜-inch (1 cm) seam allowance on all edges. Zigzag seam the straight sides on all four crown pieces.

2. Cut out a strip of fabric measuring 12 by 1½ inches (30 by 4 cm) and make a tie (page 70).

3. Pin the four crown pieces together in pairs with right sides facing and sew with a zigzag or stretch stitch if the fabric is elastic. Press the seam allowances apart and top stitch them down from the right side on both sides of the seam as shown in Fig. 3.

4. Fold the tie at midpoint and lay the tie at the center point of the crown, sandwiching it between the two crown halves. Pin and sew the two halves together as shown in Fig. 4. Press the seam allowances apart, turn right side out, and topstitch on both sides of the new seam.

5. Finish by following steps 1–4 of Alpine Skimmer.

CUTTING LAYOUT

17b

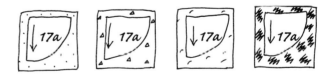

17a   17a   17a   17a

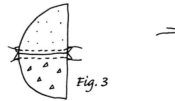

Fig. 3

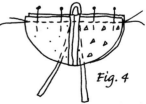

Fig. 4

AFGHAN FARMER'S HAT

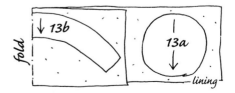

This soft hat feels great when pulled down over the ears on a cold winter day. In summer, it protects the head from the burning sun. Make it in wool or fleece for winter, or linen, cotton, or backed burlap for summer. Line with cotton, silk, or a synthetic lining fabric.

SIZES	I	II	III	IV
HS IN INCHES	21¼–22⅛	22⅛–23	23–23¾	23¾–24½
HS IN CM	54–56	56–58	58–60	60–62

MATERIALS

• 1/2 yard (.45 m) outer fabric
• 1/3 yard (.30 m) lining fabric

PATTERN PIECES

13a, Crown: Cut 1 in outer fabric and 1 in lining
13b, Stand: Cut 1 in outer fabric and 1 in lining
13c, Brim: Cut 2 in outer fabric

CONSTRUCTION

1. Pin pattern pieces to outer fabric, marking CF and CB. Add a ³⁄₈-inch (1 cm) seam allowance on all sides and cut out. Repeat in lining fabric.

2. Pin the outer fabric stand together at CB with right sides facing and sew together. Do the same with the lining stand. Press the seam allowances apart.

3. Pin and sew the two parts of the brim together with right sides facing along the outer edge. Press the seam allowances apart. Notch the seam allowance if you are working with a heavy fabric (page 70). Turn right side out and press lightly. Pin the inner edges of the brim together.

4. Pin the outer and inner stands to opposite sides of brim (sandwiching it) with right sides facing, matching the CB and CF points, along the lower edge. Sew together.

5. Pin the outer stand to the outer crown with right sides facing, matching the CB and CF points. Sew together. Lightly press the seam allowances apart.

6. Pin the lining stand to the lining crown with right sides facing, matching the CB and CF points. Sew together with ¹⁄₂-inch (1.5 cm) seam allowance, leaving a 4-inch (10 cm) opening on one side.

7. Turn right side out through the opening and sew the opening closed by hand (page 74). Smooth the lining into the hat.

CUTTING LAYOUT

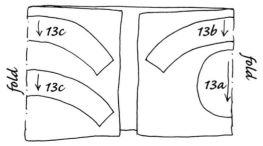

Afghan Farmer's Hats

From left to right, back row:
Gardening Hat, page 49; Baby's Bonnet, page 19; Afghan Farmer's Hat, page 46. Sixpence Hat, page 39.

From left to right, front row:
Squashy Hat, page 40; Straight Headband with bow, page 51.

GARDENING HAT 🪑🪑🪑

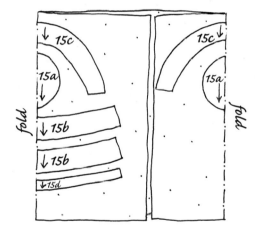

The perfect hat for when you're out gardening, fishing, or any other time in the sun. There are ventilation holes in the stand, and a snap holds the brim up. Make this hat in heavy cotton, linen, leather, denim, or corduroy.

CHILDREN'S SIZES

	I	II	III
HS IN INCHES	19¾	20½	21¼
HS IN CM	50	52	54

ADULT SIZES

	IV	V	VI	VII
HS IN INCHES	22⅛	23	23¾	24½–25¼
HS IN CM	56	58	60	62–64

MATERIALS

• Sizes I - III: ⅔ yard (.60 m) fabric
• Sizes IV - VII: ¾ yard (.70 m) fabric
• Snap fastener
• 4 eyelets

PATTERN PIECES

15a, Crown: Cut 2

15b, Stand: Cut 2

15c, Brim: Cut 2

15d, Band: Cut 1

A fabric strip measuring 1½ inches (4 cm) by the circumference of the outer edge of the brim plus a 1⅛ inch (3 cm) seam allowance

CUTTING LAYOUTS

CONSTRUCTION

1. Pin the pattern pieces to the fabric. Mark CF, CB, and the joining marks. Add a ⅜-inch (1 cm) seam allowance on all edges and cut out.

2. Fold the two stand pieces with right sides facing, and sew each, separately, at CB.

3. Press seam allowances apart and topstitch on both sides of seam.

4. Pin the double crown to the upper edge of one stand, right sides facing, matching CF, CB, and joining marks. Then pin the other stand to the other side of the crown with right sides facing so that the crown is sandwiched between the two stands.

5. Sew through all four layers. Turn right side out and press one stand down over the other. Topstitch through all layers ¼ inch (.5 cm) from seam on stand.

6. Fold the two brim pieces in half separately with right sides facing and sew together at CB.

7. Press the seam allowances apart and topstitch on both sides of the seam.

8. Pin one brim piece to the outer stand with right sides facing, matching CF, CB, and joining points. Sew.

9. Pin the other brim piece on the inner stand, and continue as in Step 8.

10. Press both seam allowances up toward the stand. Pull one hat down over the other.

11. Sew lines of topstitching around the brim at ³⁄₈-inch intervals, starting at the lower edge of the stand and proceeding to the outside edge of the brim as shown in Fig. 1.

12. Pin the strip of straight fabric to the inner brim's outer edge and bind the edge of both brims as if with bias tape (page 71).

13. Fold the hat band (15d) in half crosswise with right sides facing, and sew together at CB. Press the seam allowances apart.

14. Fold under seam allowances of both the upper and lower edges. Press. Turn right side out.

15. Pin the band to the hat at the CB and CF, covering the brim/stand seam. Sew in place ⅛ inch from band's upper and lower edges as shown in Fig. 2.

16. Set snap fastener and eyelets as marked on the pattern.

Variation

FLY FISHERMAN'S HAT

1. Follow steps 1–13 for the Gardening Hat.

2. Zigzag the hat band's long sides, then do Step 14.

3. Stitch ⅛ inch from the band's upper and lower edges.

4. Pin the band onto the hat, matching the CF and CB. Sew the band to the hat with short vertical seams all the way around, 1¾ inches (5 cm) apart. (Refer to Fig. 3.)

5. Set snap fastener and eyelets as marked on pattern.

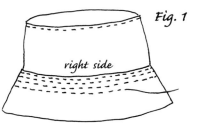

Fig. 1

right side

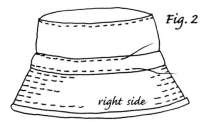

Fig. 2

right side

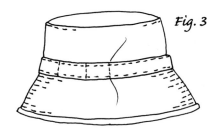

Fig. 3

STRAIGHT HEADBAND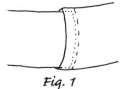

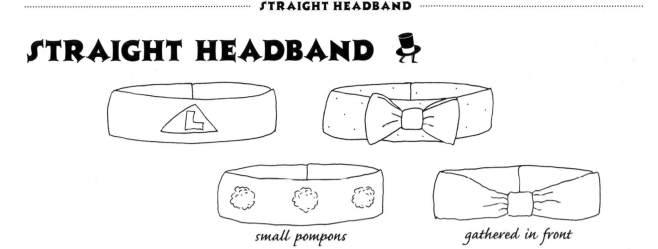

small pompons   *gathered in front*

A headband is the perfect choice when you're not in the mood for a hat but you need to keep your ears warm or your hair out of your eyes. Make the headband in fleece, cotton-lycra, or ribbing.

SIZES

Customized to wearer's head size

MATERIALS

- ¼ yard (.22 m) fleece cut to the HS long by 5½ inches (14 cm) wide, including seam allowances
- ¼ yard ribbing or cotton-lycra cut to the HS minus 4 inches (10 cm) long by 5½ inches (14 cm) wide, including seam allowance.

CUTTING LAYOUT

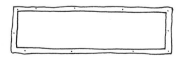

CONSTRUCTION

1. Measure HS and cut the headband directly from the fabric, using Sizes as a guide.

2. Pin and sew the headband together lengthwise with right sides facing in a short zigzag or stretch stitch.

3. Turn right side out through one end.

4. Sew the CB by inserting one end into the other and tucking the outside seam allowance inside as shown in Fig. 1. Sew together by hand (page 74).

5. Topstitch over the seam from the right side at CB.

6. Optionally, decorate with a bow (page 74), appliqué (page 69), or embroidery (page 70).

Fig. 1

EAR WARMERS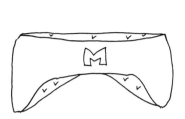

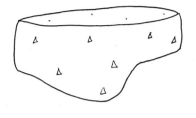

in fake fur

Ear warmers are great for keeping your earlobes toasty on a bitter day. Make them from fleece for winter or cotton-lycra for spring and fall.

SIZES	I	II	III
HS IN INCHES	19–20½	20½–22⅛	22⅛–23
HS IN CM	48–52	52–56	56–60

SIZES	IV	V
HS IN INCHES	23¾–24½	24½–25¼
HS IN CM	60–62	62–64

MATERIALS

• ⅓ yard (.30 m) fabric

PATTERN PIECES

20a, Ear Warmer: Cut 2 pieces

CUTTING LAYOUT

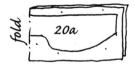 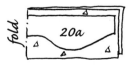

CONSTRUCTION

1. Pin pattern to fabric. Add a ⅜-inch (1 cm) seam allowance on all edges and cut out.

2. Pin the two pieces together with right sides facing and sew the two long sides together with a short zigzag stitch or stretch stitch. (Refer to Fig. 1.)

3. Turn right side out through one end.

4. Form the band into a ring by inserting one end into the other, then turning in the outside seam allowance as shown in Straight Headband project (page 51, Fig. 1.). Sew together by hand.

5. Topstitch over the hand-sewn seam at the CB.

6. Optionally, decorate the front with embroidery (page 70), an appliqué (page 69), or by sewing on a little badge or mark.

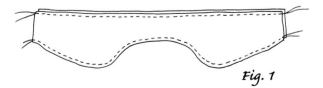

Fig. 1

RUSSIAN HAT

fur

harlequin checks

A winter hat for both men and women that looks great in fleece, wool, canvas, fur, linen, or pellon-backed burlap.

SIZES

SIZES	I	II	III	IV	V
HS IN INCHES	22	23	23½	24½	25¼
HS IN CM	56	58	60	62	64

MATERIALS

- ⅓ yard (.30 m) outer fabric
- ⅓ yard lining fabric

PATTERN PIECES

14a, Crown: Cut 1 of outer fabric and 1 of lining fabric
14b, Stand: Cut 1 of outer fabric and 1 of lining fabric

CUTTING LAYOUT

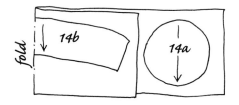

CONSTRUCTION

1. Pin the pattern pieces to the outer fabric, marking the CF and CB. Add a ⅜-inch (1 cm) seam allowance on all sides and cut out. Repeat with lining fabric.

2. Pin the outer stand together at the CB with right sides facing and sew the CB seam together. Press the seam allowances apart. Repeat in lining fabric.

3. Pin the outer crown to the outer stand, matching the CF and CB points and with right sides facing. Sew the stand to the crown. Repeat in the lining fabric, but sew ½ inch (1.5 cm) from the edges. Lightly press the seam allowances apart.

4. Turn the lining hat right side out and place inside the outer hat with the right sides facing and matching the CB points. Pin, then sew around the lower edge, leaving a 3⅛ inch (8 cm) opening. Turn the hat right side out through the opening.

5. Hand sew the opening closed (page 74). Smooth the lining hat into the outer hat. Press the lower edge lightly.

6. Optionally, topstitch the lower edge from the outside.

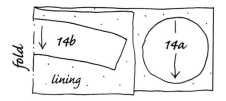

CROSS-COUNTRY SKI CAP

When the wind howls and snow flies, it's nice to pull this two-layered ski cap down over your ears. The cap works best when sewn in ribbing or jersey. If you make it in fleece, the lining should be thin jersey.

SIZES	I	II
HS IN INCHES	19–20$\frac{1}{2}$	20$\frac{1}{2}$–22$\frac{1}{8}$
HS IN CM	48–52	52–56

SIZES	III	IV
HS IN INCHES	22$\frac{1}{8}$–23$\frac{3}{4}$	23$\frac{3}{4}$–25$\frac{1}{4}$
HS IN CM	56–60	60–64

MATERIALS
• Two fabrics, each $\frac{1}{2}$ yard (.45 m)

PATTERN PIECES
18a, Ski Cap: Cut 2

CUTTING LAYOUT

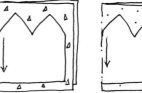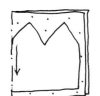

*turned up edge
and tassels*

with name appliqué

*with pompon and
embroidery*

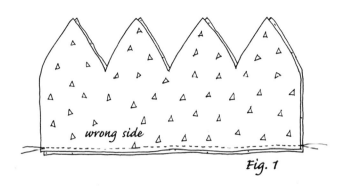

Fig. 1

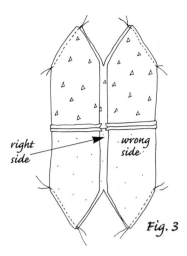

right side

wrong side

Fig. 3

CONSTRUCTION

1. Pin pattern pieces to fabrics, marking CF and CB. Add a 3/8-inch seam allowance on all edges and cut out.

2. Pin the two cap pieces together with right sides facing along the lower edge. Sew together with a short zigzag or stretch stitch as shown in Fig. 1.

3. Press seam allowances apart lightly as shown in Fig. 2.

4. Fold the cap in to the CF, one quarter from each side with right sides facing. Sew the outside diagonal edges on both ends as shown in Fig. 3.

5. Shift the fold so that the new seams are in the center and the unsewn diagonals and the open CB seam are on the sides. (Refer to Fig. 4.) Sew all seams, but leave a 3 1/8-inch (8 cm) opening in the inside cap's CB seam.

6. Turn right side out through the opening and sew the opening closed by hand (page 74).

7. Smooth the inner cap into the outer cap. Lightly press the lower edge.

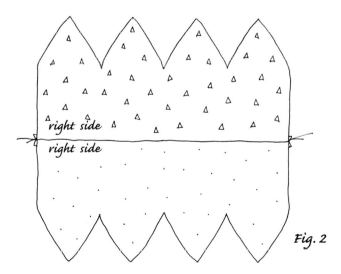

right side

right side

Fig. 2

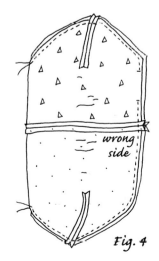

wrong side

Fig. 4

SKI PATROL HAT

in fake fur

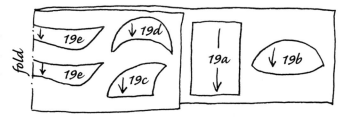

without ear flaps

This hat is great for preventing cold ears on active kids. Fleece, wool, linen, and heavy cotton fabrics are perfect for the outer fabric; choose silk or cotton for the lining.

CUTTING LAYOUTS

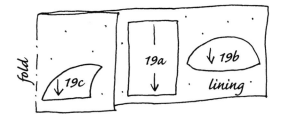

SIZES	I	II	III
HS IN INCHES	23	23¾	24½–25¼
HS IN CM	58	60	62–64

MATERIALS

- ⅓ yard (.30 m) outer fabric
- ⅓ yard lining fabric
- ⅙ yard (.15 m) iron-on interfacing

PATTERN PIECES

19a, Top: Cut 1 each in outer and lining fabrics

19b, Front: Cut 1 each in outer and lining fabrics

19c, Side: Cut 2 each in outer and lining fabrics

19d, Visor: Cut 2 in outer fabric and 4 (with no seam allowance) in iron-on interfacing

19e, Ear Flap: Cut 2 in outer fabric

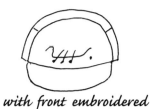

with front embroidered

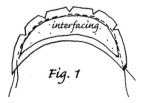

cave paintings

CONSTRUCTION

1. Pin the pattern pieces to outer fabric and transfer all markings to the fabric. Add a 3/8-inch seam allowance on all edges and cut out. Repeat in lining fabric.

2. Pin the outer sides to the outer top with right sides facing and sew together. Press seam allowances apart and topstitch them down from the right side on both sides of the seam.

3. Pin the outer front to the outer top/side unit, matching the CF and seams to the marks on the front and sew together. Lightly press the seam allowances apart, then topstitch them down from the right side.

4. Cut four visor pieces in interfacing with no seam allowance. Press two pieces of interfacing to the wrong side of each of the two outer visor pieces, matching the interfacing's edge to the seam line on the fabric.

5. Pin the two visor pieces together with right sides facing and sew along the outside curve of the interfacing. Notch (page 70) the curve. (Refer to Fig. 1.)

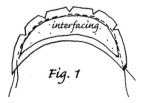

interfacing

Fig. 1

6. Turn right side out and press lightly. Topstitch 3/8 inch in from outer edge.

7. Pin the two layers of the ear flap together with right sides facing and sew the curve and lower edge. Notch the curve (page 70), turn right side out, and press lightly. Topstitch 3/8 inch in from edge.

8. Sew the lining together following Steps 2 and 3. Don't topstitch.

9. Pin the visor onto the crown unit, right sides facing, matching markings.

10. Pin the ear flap unit to the crown unit with right sides facing, matching the markings.

11. Pin the lining to the outer hat with right sides facing so that the brim and the ear flap are hidden inside the two caps. Optionally, baste the units together. Sew, but leave a 3 1/8-inch (8 cm) opening at the CB.

12. Turn right side out through the opening and press lightly. Smooth the lining into the hat and sew the opening closed by hand (page 74).

13. Optionally, zigzag a short length of narrow elastic at the CB on the ear flap.

Variation

WITHOUT EAR TABS

Cut out and assemble as described above but without piece 19e, the ear flaps

SHAWL / MUFFLER

A shawl warms your neck and shoulders and the tassels add an elegant touch. Jersey, light wools, and silk all hang well; the tassels can be made from a cotton-linen blend, wool, silk, or embroidery floss.

SIZES

FINISHED MEASUREMENTS: 60 x 30 inches (1.5 x .75 m)

Note: The muffler can be made in whatever size you wish.

MATERIALS
• 2 yards (1.8 m) fabric
• Scrap yarn for tassels

CUTTING LAYOUT

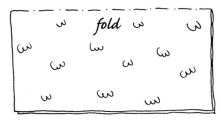

divided into four sections

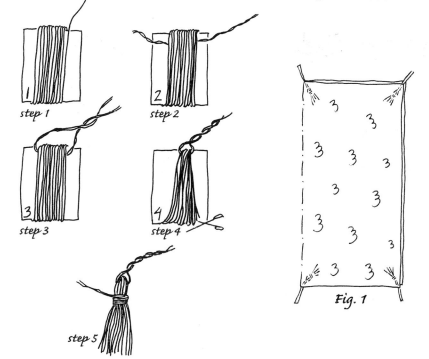

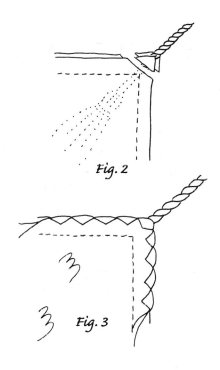

Fig. 2

Fig. 1

Fig. 3

CONSTRUCTION

1. Make 2 tassels over a 4¾-inch-wide (12 cm) piece of cardboard, winding 50 times around, following the diagrams above.

2. Trim the fabric to a 60-inch square, removing the selvages. Fold the fabric with right sides facing. Pin the tassels in the four corners, between the layers, tassel end in and cord out. Pin the edges all the way around, referring to Fig. 1. Sew with a ³/8 inch (1 cm) seam allowance on all sides, leaving a 6-inch (15 cm) opening on the long side.

3. Trim the corners as shown in Fig. 2. Turn right side out.

4. Press the right side and sew the opening closed by hand (page 74).

5. Topstitch the whole way around from the right side, ³/8 inch in from the edge. Optionally, finish with a short/wide zigzag overlapping the very edge to give a scalloped effect. (See Fig. 3.)

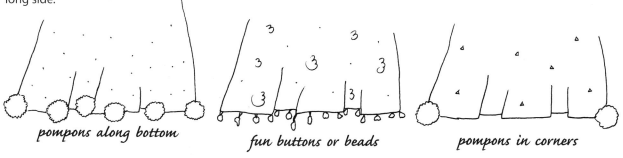

pompons along bottom　　*fun buttons or beads*　　*pompons in corners*

HOODED SHAWL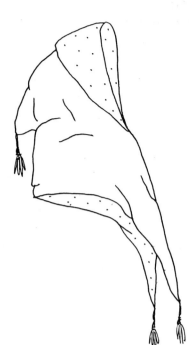

When it's cold and windy outside, this double-layered, hooded shawl is ideal. Thrown lightly around the head and shoulders, it warms you and keeps your curls in place without flattening your hair. Make it in jersey or light wools for every day, or in silk for festive occasions. The tassels can be wound in a cotton-linen blend, wool, silk, or embroidery floss.

MATERIALS

- 2²/₃ yards (2.4 m) of one fabric or 1¹/₃ yards (1.2 m) of two different fabrics
- Scrap yarn for tassels.

PATTERN PIECES

Draw a pattern on paper following the diagram below.

CUTTING LAYOUT

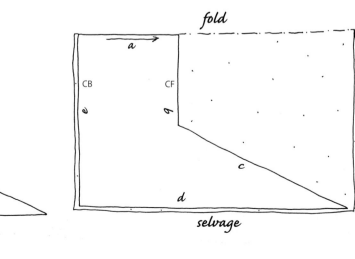

a   18 ins. (.45 m)

b   16 ins. (.40 m)

CB   CF

30 ins. (.75 m)

e

c

d
48 ins. (1.2 m)

fold

a

CB   CF

e   *q*

c

d

selvage

x 2

CONSTRUCTION

1. Trim the selvage off the fabric and pin the pattern in place, then cut out. Note: A 3/8-inch (1 cm) seam allowance is already included in the pattern.

2. Make three tassels (page 59) by winding yarn 60 times around a 4.75-inch-long (12 cm) piece of stiff cardboard.

3. Fold the outer fabric with right sides facing and pin side e together (CB). Repeat with the inner fabric.

4. Sew side e together on the inner piece with a short zigzag or stretch stitch. Press the seam allowance to the right and turn right side out.

5. Pin a tassel between the layers of the outside piece at angle a/e, tassel inside, cord out, referring to Fig. 1. Sew side e together with a short zigzag or stretch stitch.

6. Press the seam allowance to the right.

7. Lay the inner piece inside the outer piece with right sides facing to make a double shawl. (See Fig. 2.)

8. Pin inner to outer shawls at CB and sides b (CF), c (lapel), and d (lower edge).

9. Pin a tassel between the layers of each c/d corner, tassel in, cord out.

10. Sew sides b, c, and d with a short zigzag or stretch stitch, leaving a 4-inch (10 cm) opening on side d for turning. Take special care not to sew into the tassels on the narrow points.

11. Press the sides and notch angle b/c as shown in Fig. 3.

12. Trim seam allowance to 1/4 inch (.5 cm) at corners c/d. Turn right side out through the opening. Press the seams. Sew the opening closed by hand (page 74).

13. Topstitch the shawl, referring to Step 5 under Shawl/Muffler.

14. Tack the two layers together inconspicuously at corner a/e.

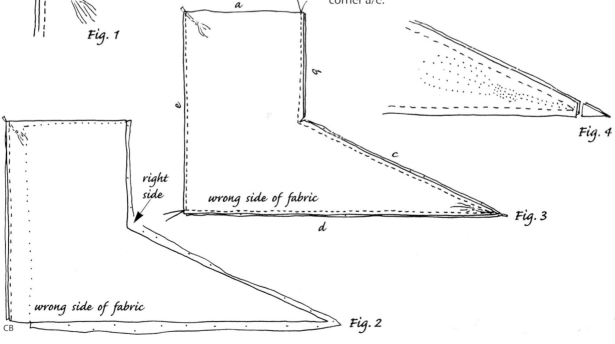

fold

Fig. 1

a

b

e

right side

wrong side of fabric

c

d

Fig. 4

Fig. 3

wrong side of fabric

CB

Fig. 2

MITTENS 🎩

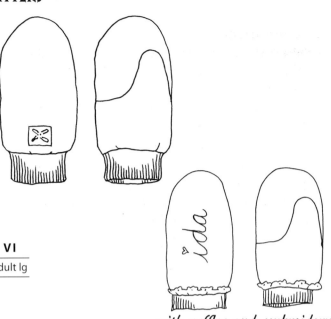

These warm mittens are easy to make for adults and children. Make them from a bright-colored fleece, optionally with windproof fabric outside and insulating fabric inside.

SIZES

I	II	III	IV	V	VI
0–2 years	2–5 years	5–10 years	adult sm	adult med	adult lg

MATERIALS

- ⅓ yard (.30 m) fabric
- ¼ yard (.22 m) ribbing

PATTERN PIECES

23a, Mitten Back: Cut 2
23b, Mitten Palm and Thumb, Lower Half: Cut 2
23c, Mitten Palm and Thumb, Upper Half: Cut 2

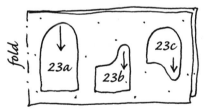

with ruffles and embroidery

CUTTING LAYOUT

CONSTRUCTION

1. Pin pattern pieces to fabric. Add a ⅜-inch (1 cm) seam allowance to all edges and cut out.

2. Sew or embroider any desired decorations on the mitten backs or above the cuffs.

3. Pin the lower palm piece and the upper palm piece together from A to B with right sides facing. Sew the center palm seam and around the thumb with a short zigzag or a stretch stitch. Trim the seam allowance somewhat and zigzag it. Remember that a pair of hands has thumbs on opposite sides.

4. Pin the mitten back and mitten palm together with right sides facing and sew from lower edge to lower edge around the hand. Trim the seam allowance a little and zigzag it.

5. For ribbed cuffs:

Children's sizes: Cut 2 pieces as wide as the wrist circumference and 4 inches (10 cm) long. (Includes seam allowances.)

Adult sizes: Cut 2 pieces as wide as the wrist circumference and 4¾ inches (12 cm) long. (Includes seam allowances.)

6. Cut the ribbing to measure 16 inches (43 cm) long by 4¾ inches (12 cm) wide. Fold and sew the ribbing together lengthwise (page 72). Pin to the lower edge of the mitten with right sides facing. Sew, stretching the ribbing a little to fit. (See Fig. 1.) Zigzag the seam allowance.

Variation

LINED MITTENJ

1. Cut out the pieces in both outer and lining fabrics. Follow Steps 1–5 in both lining and outer fabrics, leaving a 2½ inch (6 cm) opening in the lining side seam for turning.

2. Sew the ribbing into a ring (page 72). Pin to the lower edge of the mitten with right sides facing. Place the outer mitten and lining right sides facing with the ribbing sandwiched between them. Sew with a short zigzag or a stretch stitch.

3. Turn the mittens right side out through the opening and hand stitch the opening closed (page 74). Smooth the lining mitten into the shell to make a double mitten.

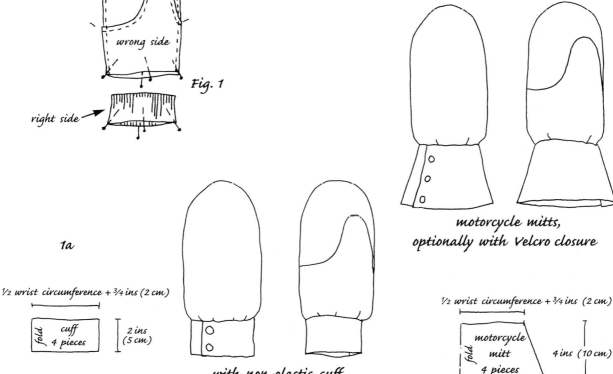

wrong side

Fig. 1

right side →

1a

½ wrist circumference + ¾ ins (2 cm)

fold | cuff | 4 pieces

2 ins (5 cm)

with non-elastic cuff, optionally with velcro closure

motorcycle mitts, optionally with Velcro closure

½ wrist circumference + ¾ ins (2 cm)

fold | motorcycle mitt | 4 pieces

4 ins (10 cm)

½ wrist circumference + 1½ ins (4 cm)

TOOLS

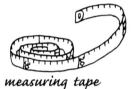

dressmaker's pins

Dressmakers pins: Use fine straight pins to avoid the holes left in fine fabrics by heavy pins.

tailor's ham

Tailor's pressing ham: Makes it easier to press curved seams (page 72).

measuring tape

Measuring tape: Used, among other things, for measuring head sizes.

press cloths

Press cloths: If you don't have a steam iron, you can use a damp, clean cotton cloth (a piece of old sheet or a dish towel, for example) to put between the iron and the fabric.

seam ripper

Ripper: A necessity for ripping out mistaken seams.

tailor's chalk and pencil

Tailor's chalk or tailor's pencils: Used to make removable markings on fabric. Always try removing a sample mark on a scrap piece of fabric before writing on your main fabric.

paper scissors

Paper scissors: To cut out patterns.

dressmaker's shears

Shears: Good quality, sharp shears to be used only on fabric are a must.

Sewing machine needles: Choose sewing machine needles based on the fabric you are using.

iron

Iron and ironing board: For pressing seams and finished garments.

needle and thread

Hand sewing needles: You will need needles of different gauges for different types and weights of fabric. Choose a thin gauge needle for light fabrics and thicker gauge needles for heavier fabrics.

sewing machine

Sewing machine: For most of the designs in this book, you will need a zigzag machine with a free arm. If your machine has a stretch seam, so much the better. Use it when called for in the sewing directions.

FABRICS

LACES

Laces are often a blend of cotton and synthetic fibers. They form an open "weave" with patterns and are available in different colors. Can be used on hats and visored caps.

COTTON-LYCRA

A blend of cotton and synthetic fibers, cotton-lycra is usually 90 percent cotton and 10 percent lycra. The fabric is very elastic and soft, and is available in many colors and patterns. Can be used for elastic caps and as a lining for winter caps.

HEAVY COTTONS

These fabrics are well-suited to hats that need some stiffness (body). Available in different plain colors and with printed patterns.

FLEECE

This fabric is most often knitted of synthetic fibers with a brushed surface that is warm, soft, and elastic. It is available both in solid colors and patterned surfaces. Good for all kinds of winter caps, hats, and mittens.

CORDUROY

Corduroy is available with narrow and wide wales. Pinwale, with tiny wales (baby corduroy), is 100 percent cotton and very soft. Wide-waled, heavy trouser corduroy is often a polyester-cotton blend. Take care that the pile is in the right direction before you cut. The handsome, dark colors show only when the pile is pointed upward (the opposite direction from your dog's fur). The fabric should feel smooth when stroked from bottom to top. Corduroy is available in many colors and sometimes in printed patterns. Use it for visored caps and hats.

BURLAP

This natural fabric is made of jute fibers. Stiff, coarse, and loosely woven in its natural yellow-tan color, it's nice for a summer hat.

LINEN

A natural fiber from flax plants, linen is often blended with cotton or rayon. Linen has a cool touch and a light sheen; it wrinkles easily and is never elastic. Linen makes a great summer or visored hat. Available in many colors, both plain, patterned, or striped.

JERSEY

This soft, light, and somewhat stretchy fabric is knitted circularly by machine. It can be purchased in 100 percent cotton or in a synthetic blend. Available in many solid colors and patterns, jersey is good for mufflers, as lining material, or for summer caps.

GROSGRAIN RIBBON

A tightly woven ribbon with prominent weft ribs. Available in different widths and colors.

RIBBING

A knitted blend of cotton and synthetic fibers that is very elastic. Use better qualities with a good "memory;" avoid ribbings that lose their stretch quickly. Ribbing is available in solids and patterns, and is used for winter caps, ear warmers, headbands, and edgings.

SILK

A natural fiber, silk is wonderfully comfortable to wear. Light and firmly woven, it hangs elegantly.

LEATHER

Most often calf, sheep, or lambskin, leather is windproof and has a smooth, shiny surface. It is available in many colors and is useful for visored caps and hats. We recommend a little practice sewing before you launch into working with leather. Once you have sewn a seam wrong and ripped it, you will never get rid of the needle holes. Before you start, make up the pattern in an inexpensive piece of cotton to be sure the hat design fits and becomes you.

Don't pin the pieces together, as pins will make unremovable holes in the leather. Instead, use clips or tape. Sew with a leather needle or use a teflon foot on your sewing machine.

It's a good idea to take your pattern pieces with you when shopping for leather so you can purchase exactly the right amount.

Remember to have the pattern pieces oriented for right and wrong sides, so that your pieces are cut in the correct direction. You can recycle an old leather jacket or coat into hats as well.

Don't iron leather; use your fingernail or the flat edge of your scissors to press the seam allowance apart.

BIAS TAPE

Bias tape is cut on the diagonal of woven fabric so that it can be used for binding curves. It is available in several widths and many colors.

STRETCH VELOUR

A soft, elastic knit with pile on the right side, stretch velour is a blend of cotton and synthetic fibers. Work with stretch velour in the same way as corduroy when cutting. It is available in many colors, and is good for pointed hats, ski caps, hoods, bonnets, and more.

SEAM TAPE

This woven tape with selvages on both edges is used to stiffen edges and make them less elastic. It is available in various widths and colors.

WOOL

A natural fiber used either alone or in blends with polyester. Wool is valued for its abilities to warm and to absorb dampness from the body. It is available in plain colors, checks, plaids, and tweeds, and in various weights and forms. Wool makes an ideal outer fabric for winter hats.

VELOUR

A blend of cotton and synthetic fibers or 100 percent cotton, velour is a woven fabric with a soft pile on the right side. Velour is cut following the same rules as corduroy. It is available in many colors and weights and is great for hats and visored caps.

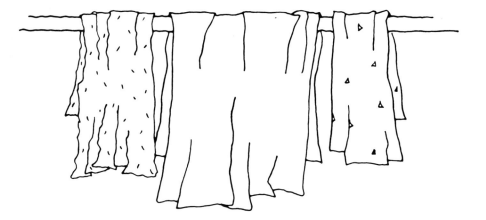

SEWING TIPS

APPLIQUÉ

1. Make a sketch of the motif on paper as shown in Fig. 1-1.

2. Transfer the drawing to a piece of fusible web, drawing on the adhesive side in order not to have the motif in mirror image on the hat. (Refer to Fig.1-2.)

3. Cut out the motif with about a ³⁄₈-inch (1 cm) seam allowance as shown in Fig. 1-3.

4. Iron the fusible web motif onto the wrong side of the fabric. Press onto the paper with the glue side toward the fabric. (Refer to Fig. 1-4.)

5. Cut out in paper following your original outline as shown in Fig. 1-5.

6. Peel off the paper and place the motif on the hat or cap. Iron the motif in place, then sew around the edges with a tight zigzag stitch as shown in Fig. 1-6. Reduce the length of the zigzag as you approach corners to reduce bulk. (Refer to Fig. 2.)

Fig. 1

interfacing

wrong side

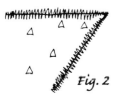

Fig. 2

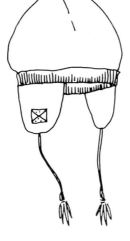

TIES

1. For a ¼-inch-wide (.5 cm) tie, cut a piece of fabric along the grain 14 inches (45 cm) by ¾ inch (2 cm), which includes seam allowance.

2. Fold the fabric lengthwise with right sides facing.

3. Cut a 20-inch-long (50 cm) cotton string and lay it between the two layers of fabric. Pin it fast to one end of the fabric, then pin the rest of the fabric together.

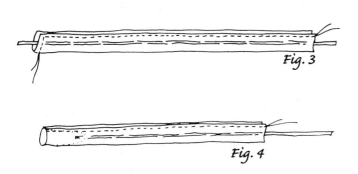

Fig. 3

Fig. 4

4. Sew across the end, then along the open side, a presser foot's width in, and taking care not to sew into the string. (Refer to Fig. 3.)

5. Trim seam allowance.

6. Carefully pull the fixed end of the string through the tie. Help get it started by folding fabric in at the fixed end as shown in Fig. 4.

7. Keep pulling until the fabric is right side out. Cut off the string. Tuck the seam allowance in at the other end and close the end with hand stitching.

EMBROIDERY

Embroidery can be effective on visored caps, ear warmers, and on the ear flaps of the Inca cap. The chain stitch (Fig. 5) and the stem stitch (Fig. 6) are simple to learn and easy to do.

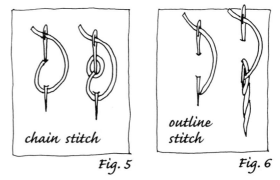

chain stitch

outline stitch

Fig. 5   *Fig. 6*

NOTCHING CURVES

To keep curved seams from pulling when they are right side out, cut little notches in the seam allowance as shown in Fig. 7.

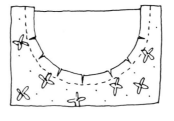

Fig. 7

BINDING EDGES

1. For a 3/8-inch-wide (1 cm) binding, cut a strip with the grain of fabric that is 1 1/2 inches (4 cm) by the circumference of the hat plus 3/4 inch (2 cm) including the seam allowance.

2. Press in the long sides 3/8 inch on each side so that the edges meet in the middle. (Refer to Fig. 8.)

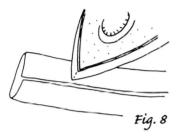

Fig. 8

3. Open the folds out and fold one end 3/8 inch toward the wrong side. Pin the strip to the lower edge of the brim with right sides facing, placing the folded end at the CB. Place and pin the strip around the entire brim, letting the end cover the folded end. (Refer to Fig. 9.)

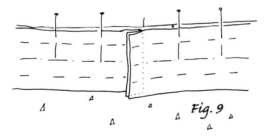

Fig. 9

4. Stitch the strip on at the lengthwise fold line. Trim seam allowances, then turn the tape up around the edge of the brim, tucking the seam allowance under at the lengthwise fold. Pin and stitch 1/8 inch from the tape's folded edge as shown in Fig. 10.

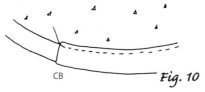

CB   *Fig. 10*

POMPON

1. Cut out two cardboard circles with a hole in the middle and a cut in the side as shown in Figure 11. Or use the pompon template pattern 24a. The pompon will have the diameter of the template, in this case 2 inches (5 cm).

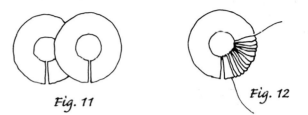

Fig. 11   *Fig. 12*

2. Place the templates together, with the cut in the same position, and wind the yarn around them, densely and uniformly. Figure 12.

3. When the hole is completely filled, cut the yarn between the edges of the two templates. Figure 13.

4. Wrap a string (or matching yarn) 5 or 6 times around the yarn, between the templates, tightly, and tie a knot. Remove the templates. Figure 14.

Fig. 13   *Fig. 14*

5. Trim the pompon. Optionally, steam it over a kettle of boiling water to fluff the cut ends of yarn.

Fig. 15

A SIMPLE TAILOR'S PRESSING HAM

A tailor's pressing ham can simplify the pressing of curves. It is simple to make and can be used on a table or an ironing board.

1. Cut a piece of firm fabric to a 24-inch square (60 cm) (includes seam allowance).

2. Fold the piece in quarters and press the folds as shown in Fig.16.

3. Unfold one fold, so the fabric is still doubled. Measure 3 inches (8 cm) from both sides of the center fold and fold the corners down at a right angle. Press in place. Open these corner folds and machine stitch on the fold lines with short, straight stitches as shown in Fig. 17. Fasten the thread ends firmly.

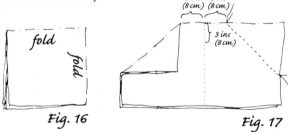

Fig. 16   *Fig. 17*

4. Repeat Step 3, with the fabric folded in the opposite direction, along the other set of fold lines.

5. Trim seam allowances to $3/8$ inch (1 cm). Turn right side out.

6. Fill the bag with fine sand to a height of 5 inches (13 cm).

7. Tie strong cotton string tightly around the top. (Refer to Fig. 18.)

8. Turn the corners down to one side, turn the seam allowance under, and sew the corners to the bag by hand as shown in Fig. 19.

9. Your pressing ham can be used with the tie up or down.

Fig. 18   *Fig. 19*

RIBBING

1. Cut ribbing in the desired width. The length is determined by the size of the head, or whatever body part the ribbing will encompass.

2. Pin and sew the ribbing together, right sides facing, into a ring with a short zigzag or stretch stitch as shown in Fig. 20.

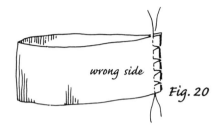

wrong side   *Fig. 20*

3. Fold the ribbing lengthwise with wrong sides facing as shown in Fig. 21.

4. Mark with pins four quarter points on both the ribbing and the edge it will be applied to.

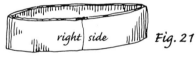

right side   *Fig. 21*

5. Turn the garment inside out and pin the ribbing in place on the inside, matching pin to pin, and placing the seam at the CB as shown in Fig. 22.

6. Sew the ribbing on with a short zigzag or stretch seam, stitching from pin to pin. Zigzag the raw edges.

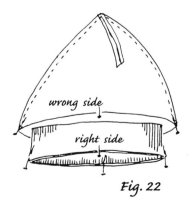

wrong side

right side

Fig. 22

ROSETTES

1. Cut two circles of fabric with a 2-inch (5 cm) radius (includes seam allowance).

2. Cut a hole with a ³⁄₈-inch (1 cm) radius in the center of both circles as shown in Fig. 23.

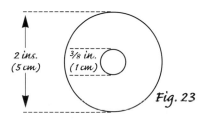

Fig. 23

2 ins. (5 cm)

³⁄₈ in. (1 cm)

3. Pin the fabric circles together with right sides facing and sew around ³⁄₈ inch from the edge.

4. Notch the seam allowance and turn right side out through the hole in the middle. Lightly press the circles.

5. Baste a gathering thread around the center hole in the circles and pull up the thread until the hole disappears. Fasten the thread end.

6. Cut a cardboard circle with a ³⁄₈-inch radius and a fabric circle with a 1-inch (2.5 cm) radius.

7. Baste a gathering thread in the outside edge of the fabric circle.

8. Lay the little fabric circle wrong side up and then lay the little cardboard circle on top. Gather the edge of the fabric until it's quite tight around the cardboard. Fasten the thread ends.

9. Sew the covered button to the center of the rosette by hand.

GATHERING THREADS, HAND SEWN

Sew a line of fine, even running stitches ³⁄₈ inch from the edge of the fabric. Pull the thread until the edge is the desired length. Stitch down and pull the gathering thread out.

GATHERING THREADS, MACHINE SEWN

1. Use the longest stitch length and a slack upper tension on the machine. Sew two lines ³⁄₈ inch apart at the edge of the fabric as shown in Fig. 24.

2. Pull both bottom threads at the same time until the fabric is the desired length. Distribute the gathers evenly and secure the thread ends as shown in Fig. 25.

3. Stitch with normal tension and stitch length between the two gathering threads, then pull out the gathering threads.

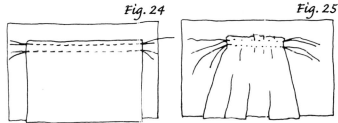

Fig. 24   Fig. 25

ZIGZAG AND STRETCH SEAMS

When sewing elastic fabrics together, you can use a short zigzag or a stretch seam. (Refer to Fig. 26.)

When zigzagging the edges of seam allowances, use a large zigzag as shown in Fig. 27.

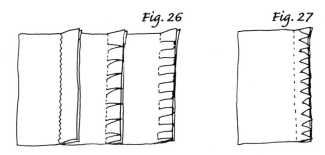

Fig. 26   Fig. 27

BOWS

1. Cut a strip of fabric (5 by 7 inches, for example) and fold it lengthwise with right sides facing. Sew the long side together, leaving a small opening at the center for turning as shown in Fig. 28.

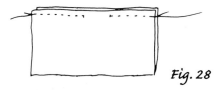

Fig. 28

2. Refold the strip lengthwise so that the seam lies at top center and sew the ends closed. (Refer to Fig. 29.)

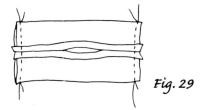

Fig. 29

3. Turn right side out, and, optionally, fill loosely with fiber fill.

4. Cut a strip of fabric measuring 1½ by 2¼ inches (4 by 6 cm). Fold in ⅜ inch on each of the long sides, wrap the strip tightly around the bow, and fasten with small hand stitches as shown in Fig. 30.

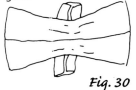

Fig. 30

5. Sew the bow onto the hat by hand.

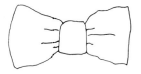

OVERHAND STITCHES

To be used when two layers of fabric are sewn together by hand (also for hems) as shown in Fig. 31.

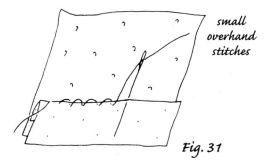

small overhand stitches

Fig. 31

INVISIBLE STITCHES

These stitches are used when two edges need to be sewn together by hand.

Sew by turn in the left and the right piece of fabric, referring to Fig. 32.

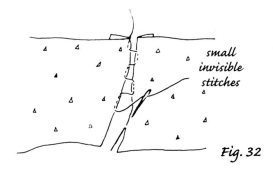

small invisible stitches

Fig. 32

SELVAGE

The outer lengthwise edge of fabric is called the selvage and shows the grain of the fabric. In elastic fabrics, it may be coated with glue to stiffen the edge. This edge should be cut off before you cut pattern pieces, if not otherwise indicated.

ALTERING PATTERNS

ALTERING BRIMS

Vertical Brims

1. Measure ½ HS. Draw perpendicularly from the CF top and bottom. Connect two CB points.

2. Measure ½ HS. Call the edge of the paper "fold line" and mark it CF. Draw a line ½ the HS long perpendicular to fold line. Draw another line from the fold line, the same length, as far from the first line as the desired height of the brim. Label the ends of the lines CB. Connect them.

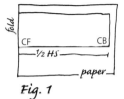

Fig. 1

hat with straight brim

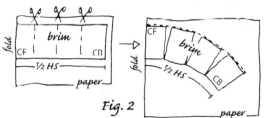

Fig. 2

Sloped Brims

1. Draft a vertical brim as directed above on paper, then cut it top to bottom into 4–6 equal segments. Spread these on a new sheet of paper in a curve so that the inside measurement remains ½ the HS and the outside line is about 10 percent larger.

2. Trace continuous lines along both inside and outside edges, as shown in Figure 2.

hat with sloped brim

hat with brim turned down

Flat Brims

1. Start with pattern for a vertical brim, but cut top to bottom into 6–8 segments. Spread these on a second sheet of paper in a partial circle until the outside measurement is 50–60 percent more than ½ the HS, but the inside still measures ½ HS.

2. Trace continuous curves both inside and out, as shown in Fig. 3.

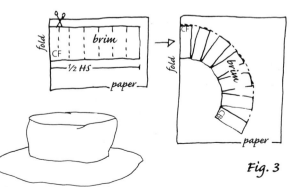

Fig. 3

hat with round brim

CHANGING THE STAND

The stand can be altered in many ways. The simplest is to alter a pattern that comes closest to what you intend. In this way, the stand can be altered without having to change other parts of the pattern.

Making the Stand Taller

Draw the stand pattern twice, either wholly or partially with one above the other, depending on the height you desire. Connect the lower CB with the upper CB as shown in Fig. 4.

Making the Stand Shorter

Trace the stand pattern on paper and pull the top (crown) edge down to the desired height. Connect the lower CB with the upper CB as shown in Fig. 5. You can also draft a new stand, but this means that you must also draft a new crown.

Making the Stand Wider

Draft a vertical stand (1/2 HS) as high as you want it. Cut it into equal pieces top to bottom and spread them on a second sheet of paper so that the bottom edge remains 1/2 the HS but the top edge has the desired width. Trace a continuous curve bottom and top to make the new pattern as shown in Fig. 6.

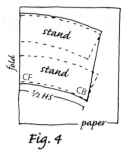

Fig. 4

hat with round brim and high stand—lining is in normal size

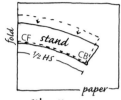

Fig. 5

hat with wide stand and sloped brim

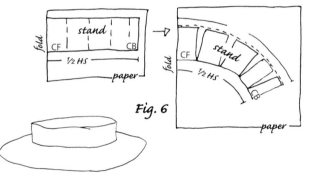

Fig. 6

hat with short stand

CROWN

When the diameter of the stand is changed, a new crown must be drafted. Measure the new circumference (remember that it is only half the circumference). The radius (1/2 the diamter) is figured by dividing the entire circumference by 16.

PATTERN SHEET TABLE OF CONTENTS

INDEX

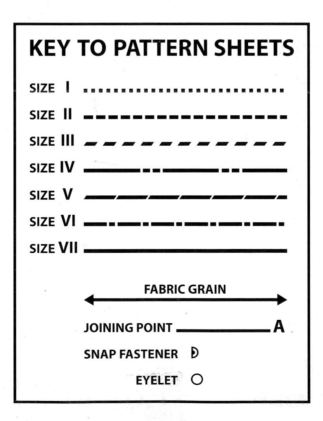

KEY TO PATTERN SHEETS

SIZE **I** ....

SIZE **II** ━ ━ ━ ━ ━ ━ ━ ━ ━ ━ ━

SIZE **III** ╱ ╱ ╱ ╱ ╱ ╱ ╱ ╱ ╱

SIZE **IV** ━━━ ‥ ━━ ‥ ━━━

SIZE **V** ━╱━╱━╱━╱━╱━╱━

SIZE **VI** ━ ▪ ━ ▪ ━ ▪ ━ ▪ ━ ▪

SIZE **VII** ━━━━━━━━━━━━

FABRIC GRAIN

⟵━━━━━━━━━⟶

JOINING POINT ━━━━ **A**

SNAP FASTENER **Đ**

EYELET ◯